# GOD

## IS MY

# BOSS

**CHARLEEN L. GOOMBS**

## PRESENTED TO

_____

## FROM

_____

## DATE

_____

# THIS BOOK IS DEDICATED TO

My nephews, who are leaders and not followers - Milton, Jr., Geoffrey, Darren, Lleyton, Joshua, Jonathan, James, Lamar, Moses, Jeremiah and Ethan-Cole.

My nieces, who are destined for greatness - Myesha, Stephanie, Jeanette, Tera-Marie, Donika, Jada, Aimee, Sidney-Brooke, Samaria and Milana.

My grand-nephews and grand-nieces, who will come to know Jesus, the power of His resurrection and the fellowship of His suffering and will become the salt of the earth - Jahmere and King Ali, Aleyeah, Mi-Angel and Nyra.

*"The Lord bless you and keep you; The Lord make His face shine upon you, and be gracious to you; The Lord lift up His countenance upon you, and give you peace." (Number 6:24-26)*

# ACKNOWLEDGMENTS

I want to take this time to acknowledge and thank God who is the Head of my life, the Lover of my soul and the Lifter up of my head. I could not have completed this devotional without the Holy Spirit. He has shown me, me. The reflection was not as pleasant. He led me in the areas to focus on by depositing a little here and a little there into my spirit from time to time during my meditation. He reminded me of the **_many_** areas I need to develop. He has truly been my guide, especially in the areas that required transparency.

To Him alone be the praise, glory and honor. Hallelujah. Thank you, Jesus.

# TABLE OF CONTENTS

# SALVATION SCRIPTURES

*"For all have sinned, and come short of the glory of God." **Romans 3:23***

*"For the Son of man is come to seek and to save that which was lost." **Luke 19:10***

*"That if thou shalt confess with thy mouth the Lord Jesus, and shalt believe in thine heart that God hath raised Him from the dead, thou shalt be saved." **Romans 10:9***

*"For with the heart man believeth unto righteousness; and with the mouth confession is made unto salvation." **Romans 10:10***

*"He that believeth and is baptized shall be saved; but he that believeth not shall be damned." **Mark 16:16***

*"For God so loved the world (you), that He gave his only begotten son, that whosoever believeth in Him should not perish but have everlasting life."* **John 3:16**

*"Go ye therefore, and teach all nations, baptizing them in the name of the Father, and of the Son, and of the Holy Ghost."* **Matthew 28:19**

*"When they heard this, they were baptized in the name of the Lord Jesus."* **Acts 19:5**

Father, in the name of Jesus, I now know that all have sinned and come short of the glory of God. I admit that I am a sinner. I believe that Your Son, Jesus, died on the cross to take away my sins and rose from the dead. I come to you with a humble heart and ask You to cleanse me of all unrighteousness. I call upon the name of Jesus Christ to be my Savior, Lord of my life, Lover of my soul and Lifter up of my head. Come into my heart. Fill me with the power of the Holy Spirit. I now believe that I am saved in Jesus. Thank You Jesus. Amen.

# PREFACE

This devotion is a matter of the heart based on what I have experienced and all of the reflection that I did. The main purpose of this book is to help my readers view the workplace through God's eyes and not theirs. My goal is to encourage you in the workplace, to put a smile on your face as you read and ponder, and to make you think and do right in the sight of God and not man. If you think for a minute that you are at work by yourself, I stop by to tell you, that you are not. You are never alone. God is with you, even when it feels like He is far away.

There are people working behind the scenes to remove God out of everything. It is *not* possible to do that if the Almighty, Ever-living God is in the very air we breathe. Stop and take a deep breath: God is in that deep breath you just took. You cannot hide from Him. He is Omnipresent-everywhere all the time. He is Omniscient-knows everything about you and everyone you work with. He knows every detail of your life. Awesome!

When I think about God being Omniscient, Matthew 10:30 comes to mind "***But the very hairs of your head are all numbered.***" Do you know how many strands of hair are on your head?

# INTRODUCTION

On Friday, October 7, 2011, my job was terminated effective December 30, 2011. The week before my last day on the job, my family and I went to Florida for the Christmas holiday and on our way back, the Lord dropped these verses in my spirit as I thought about being unemployed and having worked for over twenty-two plus years. *Isaiah 43:18-19 "Remember ye not the former things, neither consider the things of old. Behold, I will do a new thing; now it shall spring forth; shall ye not know it? I will even make a way in the wilderness, and rivers in the desert."* I asked, Lord, what new thing are you going to do in my life? I had a little talk with my Maker on that long drive back.

I was unemployed two and a half years. During that period, I went back to school full-time, obtained my degree in Business Administration and spent "quality" time with my family. God gave me enough time to reflect on the "workplace". I reflected on all the jobs I have ever held, mostly, the ones after I accepted Jesus Christ as my Lord and Savior back in April 2000. I thought about what I did wrong on those jobs and what I could have done better. After the reflection, I started confessing, Lord, when I get back in the workplace, it is not going to be business as usual. This little light of mine is going to shine one way or another. Not by might, nor by power, but by the Spirit.

During the summer of 2014, I felt in my spirit to work on a devotion for the workplace. I started this devotion, got half-way done and stopped. In the summer of 2015, the devotion came back to my mind. I started writing about the topics I was having challenges in and as I wrote, the Lord helped me along the way with other topics. In September 2015 other challenges came about and in 2016 I gave birth to *30 Days Of PRAYER For Your Employer.*

Think with me for a minute. We spend more time at work Monday through Friday, and even weekends sometimes, than we do with our family. I have learned, and I have not mastered the art of this known fact yet, that we are in control of how we react to any given situation on the job. Over the years, I have encountered all types of bosses, office managers and co-workers. You have too. There are so many people working today that are very unhappy on the job. Whether it is you, your boss, the work load, the co-workers, or any other challenges, let us strive to have peace in the midst of any storm that arises and learn how to better handle the different challenges that come our way. Think with me for a second. All those different personalities together Monday through Friday, and often, not on one accord. I am growing in grace and the knowledge of God and I have come to realize that ALL things (the good, the bad and the ugly) work together for good to them that love God, to them who are the called according to his purpose. You are on your job for a reason and a season and your due season will come. Just hold on a little longer. God told us in *Ecclesiastes 3:1* that "*there is a time for everything under the sun.*"

We encounter challenges with other Christians on the job as well. We are there to pray for the one who challenges us and work out our own salvation with fear and trembling. Remember, we have our faults too. We are not at work to preach, we are there to work and exercise Godly wisdom which is from above. We are not there to walk around saying thus said the Lord, *I Peter 1:16*, for it is written, be ye holy because I am holy, or thus saith the Lord, *Matthew 12:34*, O generation of vipers…, you get what I am saying? Don't lie on

God. God is a God of order and everything concerning Him must be done decently and in order. He is not the Author of confusion. Also, He did not send us on the job to walk around speaking in tongues loudly so everyone in the office can hear us, so don't do that either. Hear ye me, please exercise Godly wisdom.

If your job is "perfect", this devotion is not for you. If you do not have or face any challenges on your job, this is not for you. If your boss, office manager and co-workers are perfect every day and you are singing "because I'm happy"* every day, this is not for you. This devotion is for the ones who, like myself, have gone through and might still be going through different challenges in the workplace and are just thankful for God's daily grace from day to day. I believe with every fiber of my being that it is possible for us to view the workplace in God's eye view. Doing so will bring about a change in our attitudes and actions. We cannot change some situations on our job, but we can change how we "react" to those situations. Some of the topics in this devotion are areas I had challenges in, some I still have challenges in and some the Lord dropped in my spirit as I wrote this devotion.

Someone I know very well was with her company for 13 years and she had to resign because she felt that if she did not, she would have had a nervous breakdown. She sought the Lord, stepped out on faith, resigned and started a new job approximately two months later. She knew her season was up. We cannot, by any means, set out to live according to the word of God in our own strength. I fail every time I try. We have to rely daily on the Holy Spirit to be our guide. The word of God is a lamp unto our feet and a light unto our path. When the pressure hits us, we have to seriously gird up the loins of our minds and go back to the Word. I am saying for myself the exact words Brother Paul said in *Philippians 3:13-14: "Brethren, (readers), I do not count myself to have apprehended; but one thing I do, forgetting those things which are behind and reaching forward to those things which are ahead, I press toward the goal for the prize of the upward call of God in Christ Jesus.*" This is the reason why I have decided to be transparent with you and invite you on this journey with me, so God can perfect that which concerns us. I have not yet arrived. If I were to say that I have it all together, it would be a lie and I would need you to lay hands on me in the spirit, right now, and bind up that lying spirit far from me. I am not sure where you are on your journey to make a difference in the workplace, but I do know that there is always room for improvement in how we conduct ourselves in the workplace. Can I get an Amen? My sincere desire is for God alone to get the glory at the end of each work day, and yours should be too. Does He always gets the glory from my actions on the job? Nope.

Right now, I want to encourage you to seriously make a conscious effort to thank God every morning for the opportunity to serve Him in the workplace. Ask the Holy Spirit to be your guide in the things concerning work. He will guide you. Sometimes we wake up not wanting to go to work because of what or who we have to face when we get there. Been there. However, regardless of whether or not we like our job or the people on our job, we ought to love them, no matter what, and as God commanded us, give thanks for them. I believe the people on our job who rub us the wrong way are there to refine our character. I have been on the other side, rubbing others the wrong way. Am I there now? I don't know, I possibly could be rubbing someone the wrong way and not even be aware of it. The Holy Spirit is our guide. We will set out to work as unto the Lord, until our change comes. I encourage us to pray for our boss/bosses, and pray that they too will realize that they are the little boss, working for a big Boss. Pray for the success of the firm/ company/ organization etc., you are a part of. I also encourage you to pray for everyone who is a part of the firm/ company/ organization you work for, from top to bottom. God gave them the vision to start their firm/ company/ organization, etc., so you and I could be employed. So say this with me now, THANK YOU JESUS for being employed. Now, didn't that feel great?

Any challenges we encounter on the job, we should consult GOD, first. Sometimes, out of habit, we talk to our spouse, friends or even co-workers before seeking God first. Please resist the urge to do so and develop a habit of talking to God first, so He can guide you. The job is not our source. God is our Source. The job is only a resource. God opened the door for us to work as unto Him so we can provide for our family and glorify Him while we work. Every morning we wake up, I challenge us to give God thanks for being employed. We sometimes take that for granted. I do too.

God is the Boss of bosses, the Manager of managers, the Co-worker of co-workers, like He is the King of kings and the Lord of lords. I pray that this devotion will give you another view point in the things concerning the workplace and overall in any given situation on or off the job. We are on the job to change the atmosphere. God bless you, atmosphere changer.

*Because I'm Happy by Pharrell Williams (public domain)

# VOW

I _____, vow on this _____ day
of _____, 20____ that I will, not by might nor by
power, but by the Spirit, trust God to help me to
live His Word in the workplace, so He alone can
get the glory, praise and honor. Thank you Lord
for perfecting that which concerns me; Thy mercy
oh Lord, endures forever. *Psalm 138:8.*

# DECREE AND DECLARE

*"Thou shalt also decree a thing, and it shall be established unto thee: and the light shall shine upon thy ways." Job 22:28*

I, _____, decree and declare that my best days are before me, my future is bright, my latter days will be greater than my former days. I am a doer of the Word and not only a hearer. I am blessed and highly favored. If God be for me, who can be against me? I am disciplined, self-controlled and not a follower but a leader. I am what God says I am and I can do what God says I can do. I have understanding. I claim a retentive memory, I have clarity and exercise Godly wisdom in situations on my job. God's grace is sufficient to keep me. I forgive and I respect others. I am slow to anger and have mercy on others as God has mercy on me.

Hallelujah. Hallelujah. Hallelujah. Glory! Thank You Jesus. Amen!

# THE FIRST AND PERFECT BOSS

*"In the beginning God created the heaven and the earth." Genesis 1:1*

Have you ever sat and thought about who the first boss was? Can you tell, I did? The first Boss was God, as He was the first Builder and Surgeon. He was the first, everything. *John 1:1-3 "In the beginning was the Word, and the Word was with God, and the Word was God. The same was in the beginning with God. All things were made by him; and without him was not anything made that was made."* God created work and His first employee was the "man", Adam. In *Genesis 2:15*, the word says, *"And the LORD God took the man, and put him into the garden of Eden to **work** it and to keep it."* Adam had work to do. It did not say that he

19

was in the garden bench pressing, doing squats and sit-ups, trying to get a six pack, or pull-ups and push-ups working on biceps and triceps. He was working. If you read further down into verse 16, you will see that "the Garden" was not small by any means. It reads thus, "and the Lord God commanded the man, you are free to eat from any tree in the garden."

When you think about a garden, you are not really thinking about trees, are you? When I read, garden, I thought of flowers only. So that tells us that it was no ordinary Garden, because it had some trees in there. Verse 8-9 says, "Now the Lord God had planted a garden in the east, in Eden; and there he put the man he had formed. The Lord God made all kinds of trees grow out of the ground—trees that were pleasing to the eye and good for food." The key words are "all kinds of trees."

Because He is the same yesterday, today and forever, He is our Boss now and will always be. He is the Perfect Boss, so that makes Him, the Boss of bosses. He is the great Architect of this Universe (as I heard my dad once pray, years before I was even saved). When we truly understand who we are working for, the big Boss and not so much the boss, it makes a difference in our performance on the job. God sees everything we do on the job. *2 Chronicles 16:9b* said it best, *"For the eyes of the Lord run to and from throughout the whole earth, to show Himself strong on behalf of those whose heart is loyal to Him."*

We serve a God who is Omnipresent, He is everywhere at the same time. Our boss can only be in one place at a time. Hallelujah! Our boss does not see what we are doing most of the time, but our heavenly Boss does. If we are cutting corners, He sees us. If we are surfing the internet, He sees us. If we are texting, emailing, tweeting, insta-gramming, snap-chatting and face-booking all day, He sees us. We cannot Hide from God. In one of

Michael Jackson's song, he said "I always feel like some body's watching me, ain't got no privacy."* Yes, someone is watching us. We really have no privacy. The Psalmist said it better in *Psalm 139:7-10. "Where can I go from Your Spirit? Or where can I flee from Your presence? If I ascend into heaven, You are there; If I make my bed in hell, behold, You are there. If I take the wings of the morning, and dwell in the uttermost parts of the sea, even there Your hand shall lead me, and Your right hand shall hold me."* We need to develop that constant awareness of knowing He is watching us.

Those scripture verses came alive in 2001 when my two friends and I went on a Caribbean cruise. I remembered I had been saved only a year, but I had heard those verses in a church service. One evening we were at the tail end of the ship and I leaned over and said, "Lord, you are right here with us." Those scriptures came back to my memory and I smiled and was in awe. I was looking across the ocean. No sign of land-just us on this huge ship in the middle of the ocean-and it felt so good just knowing God was there with us. No worry or fear, just in awe.

Recently, the Lord brought those same scriptures to my memory to apply it to this devotion. I just want to say, Thank you Lord for the reminder. The Boss of bosses wants our light to shine, not just in the workplace, but everywhere we go. God is just awesome in each one of us. He will continue to get the praise, glory and honor. Hallelujah. Hallelujah. Hallelujah! Thank you, Jesus. *Philippians 1:6 "Being confident of this very thing, that he which hath begun a good work in you will perform it until the day of Jesus Christ."*

*Somebody's Watching Me by Michael Jackson (public domain)*

# WORK AS UNTO THE LORD

*"And whatever you do, whether in word or deed, do it all in the name of the Lord Jesus, giving thanks to God the Father through him." Colossians 3:17*

Sometimes we work and go above and beyond so we can get the glory, working to please the ones who can see us: our bosses, co-workers and office managers. That is not what God made us to do. Yes, sometimes it feels great when your boss or a co-worker says, "great job"! There is absolutely nothing wrong with feeling good about receiving a compliment for what you have accomplished. The danger in that is when you take the credit for yourself, thinking you did that "great job" in your own strength. When you acknowledge God in your deeds, it keeps you humble and He gets the glory. He tells us in *Ephesians 6:6 "Work hard, but not just to please your masters when they are watching. As **slaves of Christ**, do the will of God with all your heart."* Not as slaves for your boss, but as slaves for Christ. Work with enthusiasm, as though you were working for the Lord, rather than for people.

## *Prayer*

Most Worshipful Father, I bless, honor, praise and appreciate You. Thank You for this opportunity to serve in the workplace. Help me in whatsoever I do, to do it heartily, as to the Lord and not unto man, so You can be glorified. Help me to be strong and do not let my hands be weak, for my work shall be rewarded by You. These mercies I ask in Jesus' name. Amen.

# ACRONYMS

## E.M.P.O.W.E.R.

Encourage and

Motivate each other

Praise instead of criticize

Overcome adversity and be

Willing to listen

Empathize and show

Respect

## R.E.S.P.E.C.T.

Reason together

Effectively coaching others

Stay

Positive

Express gratitude and be

Careful how you handle each other and

Think before you speak

## H.O.N.O.R.

Have respect for

Others

Never gossip

Or

Retaliate

## ARE YOU READY?

## LET'S DO THIS!

*"In the same way, let your light so shine before men, that they may see your good works, and glorify your Father which is in heaven."*
*Matthew 5:15*

*Let us "light up" the workplace*

*Glory! Hallelujah.*

## BEGINNING PRAYER

Hallelujah. Hallelujah. Hallelujah! Lord, today, I bless, praise, worship, appreciate, thank and adore You for being PERFECT in all Your ways. I magnify, lift You up and worship You in spirit and in truth. I bow my knees and cry HOLY, HOLY, HOLY is the Lord God Almighty, who was and is and is to come.

On this day I pray *Numbers 6:24-26 That The Lord bless everyone in the workplace and keep us; the Lord make his face shine on us and be gracious to us; the Lord turn his face toward us and give us peace. Psalm 90:17 May the favor of the Lord our God rest on us; establish the work of our hands for us-yes, establish the work of our hands. I Peter 5:10 And the God of all grace, who called us to his eternal glory in Christ, after we have suffered a little while, will himself restore us and make us strong, firm and steadfast. Philemon 1:25 The grace of the Lord Jesus Christ be with our spirit in this workplace today.* In Jesus' name we pray. Amen!

# ANGER

*"Be not hasty in thy spirit to be angry: for anger resteth in the bosom of fools." Ecclesiastes 7:9*

Whenever I hear someone quote this verse or I read it for myself, a smile comes to my face because I remember some years ago, I was having so many challenges with my department heads and others in the registrar's office at the University I attended. I was in my final semester and four weeks away from earning my degree. While sitting in the library getting ready for an exam, I took a break, checked my e-mail and read an e-mail which stated that I had two more classes to take. This meant I would not have finished until December 2013, and I was livid. I got right into the flesh.

Think with me for a moment. Imagine you went to school, took five or six classes per semester, attended all year, and now in your last semester, while you're excited and looking forward to finishing up, you receive an email stating you have two more classes to complete. Now for a truth moment: how would you have reacted? I was angry and fussed with all the department heads who were involved in the process from beginning to end. I went back and forth to the different departments showing them all the classes I was told I needed to take, which I already took. In the middle of my fussing and getting angry, I called my husband to fuss some more, did not get him, and was upset I got his voice mail. I then called my cousin and let it all out. He listened and said, "lets pray." Then he gave me some encouragement and I went and took my test. The Lord reminded me of the verse above. You know what I had the nerve to say after that reminder? I ain't no fool; those people are the fools. That is the God we serve. We cannot argue with the word. It took about three days or so to clear up, but it did clear up and I had to go and apologize to the ones I had fussed at. I knew God worked it out for me, and I did finish up in August 2013 as planned.

So it is in the workplace. We encounter people who can make us really angry. This is why we need the Word of God in our hearts and not only in our minds. He will bring it back to our memory and it is now up to us to do what the Word says to do. Our responsibility is to refrain from anger, and forsake wrath. We must fret not ourselves because it tends only to evil. If we are slow to anger, it means we have great understanding, but if we have a hasty temper, we lack good sense.

## _Prayer_

Lord, when I feel like I am getting angry because of something someone said or did, remind me to be quick to hear, slow to speak, slow to anger; for the anger of man does not produce the righteousness of God. In Jesus' name. Amen!

# ATTITUDE

*"Be of the same mind one toward another. Mind not high things, but condescend to men of low estate. Be not wise in your own conceits." Romans 12:16*

It is so easy for us to get an attitude these days. We get an attitude if someone does not speak to us, if we are not acknowledged, if someone sits in our favorite seat in church on a given Sunday, if someone mistreats us or if we have a copy job and the copy machine jams up 10 minutes before it is time to leave work to go to an appointment. You can start your own list of reasons why you get an attitude. In order for us to have better attitudes, we have to renew our minds in the Word daily, thinking and doing what the Word says to do. Let this mind be in us which is also in Christ Jesus and be not conform to the pattern of this world, but be transformed by the renewing of the mind.

In Daniel 3, Shadrach, Meshach and Abednego were three Hebrew men exiled into Babylon where they lived with an idolatrous King named Nebuchadnezzar. These three Hebrew men decided to remain true to their God and not bow to any graven images. If you did not bow, the penalty was death. When they were told to bow, these three brave men replied to the king, saying "O Nebuchadnezzar, we do not need to defend ourselves before you in this matter. If we are thrown into the blazing furnace, the God we serve is able to save us from it, and he will rescue us from your hand, O king. But even if he does not, we want you to know, O king, that we will not serve your gods or worship the image of gold you have set up". Their response brought them before angry Nebuchadnezzar and they were thrown in the fiery furnace. Because of their winning attitude, God miraculously delivered them from the blazing furnace they were thrown into.

Our loyalty to God should cause us to have a winning attitude in the workplace. So many things can happen on a day-to-day basis at work that can cause us to have a bad attitude.

## *Prayer*

Lord, help me to exhibit a positive work attitude daily. Give me understanding of your word. Help me to be sober and watchful in all things and to show grace where grace is needed. In Jesus' name. Amen!

# ATTITUDE
## LET'S TALK

*"And be not conformed to this world: but be ye transformed by the renewing of your mind, that ye may prove what is that good, and acceptable, and perfect, will of God." Romans 12:2*

Do you have a bad attitude? Before you answer this question, let's define attitude. Webster defines attitude as "a settled way of *thinking or feeling* about *someone or* something, typically one that is reflected in a person's *behavior."* Now that you have told the truth and shamed the devil, let's move on. It is so easy for us to get an attitude these days. We get an attitude if someone cuts us off on the highway and if we are stuck in traffic. Oh, lest

I forget, if it is too hot or too cold or it rains consistently for three or four days.

I am working on developing sensitivity to the Holy Spirit, so when I feel the bad attitude coming on, I get a quick check in my spirit to *"chill out,"* examine the situation and just have a quick talk with God (who is a mind reader), before the attitude shows on my face or comes out of my mouth. I am reminded that I did not develop a bad attitude overnight so I know I will not be able to develop a great attitude overnight either. It is a daily process, a daily renewing of the mind.

Let us purpose in our hearts one day at a time, to be aware of our attitude toward others in and out of the workplace, even in the worst of situations and let this mind be in us, which was also in Christ Jesus. Philippians 2:5.

List five (5) things/people/reasons that cause you to have a negative workplace attitude and a corresponding way to combat that issue:

| Thing/Person/Reason | | Solution |
|---|---|---|
| Example: | Short-staffed | Pray for grace to endure and for God to send the right person. |
| 1. | | |
| 2. | | |
| 3. | | |
| 4. | | |
| 5. | | |

Some things we cannot do in our own strength. When we truly realize our fidelity to God, it will cause us to have a winning attitude in the workplace. Help us Holy Ghost.

40

## ATTITUDE-CHALLENGE

*"And be not conformed to this world: but be ye transformed by the renewing of your mind, that ye may prove what is that good, and acceptable, and perfect, will of God." Romans 12:2*

I do believe I have developed a good work attitude and am working on developing an even greater work attitude. I have come a *mighty* long way, by the grace of God.

List six (6) things that cause you to have a negative workplace attitude:

1. _____

2. _____

3. _____

4. _____

5. _____

6. _____

## List six (6) ways to combat each one:

1. _____

2. _____

3. _____

4. _____

5. _____

6. _____

## List six (6) people you know, who have winning attitudes:

1. _____

2. _____

3. _____

4. _____

5. _____

6. _____

## *Prayer*

Lord, today help me to be mindful of my attitude when dealing with others at work. In Jesus' name. Amen!

# BULLYING

*"Blessed are ye, when men shall revile you, and persecute you, and shall say all manner of evil against you falsely, for my sake." Matthew 5:11*

Joseph was the second to last son, born to Jacob, whose name was changed to Israel (Genesis 35:10). Jacob loved Joseph more than the other sons because he was born to his favorite wife, Rachael, and the sons knew it. As he grew, Jacob honored him with a coat of many colors. Life quickly changed for Joseph. The harsh description of the bullying by his brothers states: "They hated him and could not speak peaceably unto him." After a few years, on one occasion when Joseph went to take lunch to his brothers, the bullying was so out of control that the opportunity arose to kill him. A plot was thwarted and resulted in his exile and years of separation from his family.

Joseph's brothers were bullies. They may have had their reasons—every bully does. But there is no excuse for bullying. Please read Genesis, chapters 37-45 for the story.

Have you ever encountered a workplace bully? I have and it was not nice. I did not know what I know now and I took matters into my own hands. As we grow in grace and in the Lord, we will be able to recognize the behavior. By their fruit we will recognize them, *Matthew 7:20*. We should never try to deal with a bully in our own strength. We must seek the wisdom of God and take action, decently and in order when prompted by the Holy Spirit. Remember, He is our guide and He will guide us into all truth. We are more than conquerors in Christ. We are called by God to overcome evil with good because we walk by faith and not by sight.

Something to also keep in mind is that "bullying" is a spirit that is operating in that person. God told us in *Ephesians 6:12 "For we wrestle not against flesh and blood, but against principalities, against powers, against the rulers of the darkness of this world, against spiritual wickedness in high places."* Therefore, whenever we come across a bully on the job, we have to pray against the spirit that is operating in that individual.

## *Prayer*

Lord, help me to never pay back evil for evil to anyone, to respect what is right in the sight of all men, to love my enemies, to do good to those who hate me, to bless those who curse me and to pray for those who spitefully use and bully me, in Jesus' name. Amen!

# CONFUSED

*"Therefore its name was called Babel, because there the Lord confused the language of the whole earth; and from there the Lord scattered them abroad over the face of the whole earth." Genesis 11:9*

We see in the above verse that God caused the first confusion to take place. Genesis 11:4 reads: And they said, Go to, let us build us a city and a tower, whose top may reach unto heaven; and let us make us a name, lest we be scattered abroad upon the face of the whole earth.

When we try to do things in our own strength, confusion will come. I am a true testimony of this truth. There were days when I was so confused, I did not know which way to turn. Someone sent me this prayer years ago: "Lord, when I am confused guide me, when I am burned out infuse me with the light of the Holy Spirit. May the work that I do and the way I do it bring faith, joy and a smile to all that I come in contact with daily."

You might be one that just never gets confused on your job, and if you are, to God be the glory. Confusion comes from lack of understanding and Lord knows, sometimes I do not understand everything that is before me. It is okay to admit that you are confused; that is a true sign of humility. When you are faced with confusion, it is the perfect time to employ the help of the Holy

Spirit. God wants us to come to him in those times, as well as in the times we are not confused.

What challenge/challenges are you facing on your job that is causing confusion? Whatever it is, take it to the Lord in prayer. He is waiting for you to come boldly to the throne of grace to obtain mercy and find help in times of need.

## *Prayer*

Lord, thank you for the Helper, the Holy Spirit, whom the Father sent, that will teach me all things and bring to my remembrance all that you have said to me. In Jesus' name. Amen!

# CONSISTENCY

*"Therefore, my beloved brethren, be ye steadfast, unmovable, always abounding in the work of the Lord, forasmuch as ye know that your labour is not in vain in the Lord." 1 Corinthians 15:58*

Daniel will be my example for consistency. Daniel could have easily avoided being thrown into the lions' den. Daniel's jealous rivals in the government of Babylon laid a trap based on his consistent practice of daily prayer to God (Daniel 6:1-9). Daniel was fully aware of their plot. He could have said, you know what, let me just pray privately for a while until things settle down. But that was not the kind of person he was.

"When Daniel knew that the writing was signed, he went home. And in his upper room, with his windows open toward Jerusalem, he knelt down on his knees three times that day, and prayed and gave thanks before his God, as was his custom since early days" (v.10). Daniel did not panic, nor bargain with God. Instead, he continued "just as he had done before" (v.10 NIV). He was not intimidated by the pressure of persecution. Daniel's desire was to only please God. When that crisis came, he did not feel the need to change his daily routine. He stayed committed to his God. He maintained a consistent prayer life and as a result, he drew strength from the Almighty God.

Who are you drawing strength from to maintain a consistent lifestyle? Consistency requires much discipline. We can be so consistent in one area and not consistent in other areas. In all our doing, we have to maintain a heavenly perspective. We should not speak one way at home and church and another way at work. We must be consistent in the things of God.

Malachi 3:6 says For I, the Lord, do not change, therefore you, O sons of Jacob, are not consumed. He is the same yesterday, today, and forever. We cannot be the same yesterday, today and forever, because we are not God but we can strive to show the same consistency when dealing with others in the workplace.

## *Prayer*

Lord, keep my actions consistent at home, at church and in the workplace. In Jesus' name. Amen!

# CRITICISM

*"Or how can you say to your brother, 'Brother, let me remove the speck that is in your eye,' when you yourself do not see the plank that is in your own eye? Hypocrite! First remove the plank from your own eye, and then you will see clearly to remove the speck that is in your brother's eye." Luke 6:42*

He told us, didn't he? I fell into this trap many times. Criticism is one of the ordinary activities of people, but on a spiritual level, nothing is accomplished by criticizing others. The Holy Spirit is the only one in the proper position to criticize, and I just love when He does it to me. He shows me what is wrong without hurting and wounding me. *"For the word of God is quick, and powerful, and sharper than any two-edged sword, piercing even to the dividing asunder of soul and spirit, and of the joints and marrow, and is a discerner of the thoughts and intents of the heart."* Hebrews 4:12.

If we really think about it, we cannot enter into fellowship with God when we are in a critical mood. Criticism serves to make us harsh, vindictive, and cruel, and leaves us with the soothing and flattering idea that we are somehow superior to others. Do not be deceived, whatever we sow, we shall reap. As soldiers of the Lord's army we should cultivate a temperament that is never critical.

How does one cultivate a temperament that is never critical? I am glad you asked. One can cultivate a temperament that is never critical by meditating on the Word of God. Let the Word take root in our hearts. This will not happen overnight, but must be developed over time. We must be constantly aware of anything that causes us to think of ourselves more highly than others.

God does not get any glory when His children criticize others.

## *Prayer*

Lord, before I criticize, help me to see the plank in my own eyes before I talk about the speck in another's eyes. In Jesus' name. Amen!

# CRITICISM-CHALLENGE

*"In all things shewing thyself a pattern of good works: in doctrine shewing uncorruptness, gravity, sincerity, sound speech, that cannot be condemned; that he that is of the contrary part may be ashamed, having no evil thing to say of you." Titus 2:7-8*

What causes a critical spirit? Make your own list. Some reasons below:

1. Negativity.

2. Insecurity.

3. Immaturity.

4. A mind that is not renewed by the Word.

Truth moment: This is between you and God. *Romans 14:10* asked us these questions: *"But why do you judge your brother? Or why do you show contempt for your brother? For we shall all stand before the judgment seat of Christ."*

1. Do you have a critical spirit?

2. How do you feel when you criticize others?

3. How do you handle criticism?

Let us take these steps to eliminate the urge to criticize others.

1. Before we criticize, let's take the time to think of our own faults.

2. When we are tempted, let's watch and pray.

3. Try to put ourselves in the shoes of the other person before we criticize. What might seem wrong to us, might seem right to the one being criticized.

4. Hold our tongue.

God is really awesome in how he is renewing our minds as we go through and meditate on these topics. To God be the glory. We will come forth as pure gold. Just bear in mind, this is not an overnight process.

## *Prayer*

Lord, thank You for reminding me that to be critical is to sow strife, disunity and discord among others. In Jesus' name. Amen!

# DECISIONS

*"Trust in the Lord with all thine heart; and lean not unto thine own understanding. In all thy ways acknowledge him, and he shall direct thy paths."* Proverbs 3:5-6

Sometimes we make foolish decisions in life, and the consequences can be very serious. Some of the best characters in the Bible made horrific mistakes, and even though God held them in high esteem, they were harshly punished. When we study some of them and observe the cause of their mistake, we can profit by them. We must be careful not to make decisions, hastily, basing our conclusions on emotions, bad information or impulses. Examples: II Samuel 11: David and Bathsheba-chaos in his family, lost a son and could not build God's temple. I Samuel 13: Saul not waiting on Samuel and lost his Kingship and anointing. A bad decision can cause us to die spiritually. Been there.

We are never alone in the decision-making process. God said to Jeremiah in *Jeremiah 33:3*, "*call unto me and I will answer and show you great and mighty things you do not know.*" That applies to us today. Some decisions we can make on our own, like purchasing a car. Should I purchase a red car vs. a white car? Should I wear a dress vs. a skirt or slacks? Should I drink coffee or tea? Should I wear my hair down or put it in a bun? Should I wear a tie vs. no tie, cufflinks vs. no cufflinks? Know what I mean? By all means, if you choose to make those decisions without consulting God, you go right ahead. He did say, acknowledge Him in *all* our ways and He will direct our paths.

In the workplace, we too have to be careful. The decisions we make, whether we are at the top of the ladder (CEO) or at the bottom, can bring repercussions to the firm / company / organization, etc., we work for. Let us seek God's wisdom in making decisions concerning our job.

## *Prayer*

Help me to not be hasty in making decisions, but to seek You first so You can direct my path. In Jesus' name. Amen!

# DISAGREEMENT

*"Remind them of these things, charging them before the Lord not to strive about words to no profit, to the ruin of the hearers." II Timothy 2:14 (NKJV)*

Paul and Barnabas had a disagreement over John Mark in Acts 15:36-41. We have disagreements on the job as well. Do we always agree with our boss, office manager and co-workers? Misunderstandings can cause disagreement. We can use language that means one thing to the hearer, but we mean something totally different. Verse 23 told us to *"avoid foolish and ignorant disputes, knowing that they generate strife."*

We must learn how important it is to have the right attitude toward those with whom we disagree. It is legitimate to disagree strongly. Jesus did that with His disciples and particularly with the hypocritical

Pharisees. Paul and John also used strong language to disagree with the false teachers.

In the workplace, we must always respect the integrity of those with whom we disagree, and avoid resentment. However strongly we express disagreement, there is no excuse for not showing courtesy and kindness to the one we are in disagreement with. We should make sure we are careful to check what our his/her/their views really are, so we don't misrepresent them.

List some things you disagree with in the workplace. Are the reasons for disagreement legitimate reasons? Is it worth working up a sweat over?

### *Prayer*

Lord, whatever our disagreements, help me to never create division in the workplace over issues. Rather, help me to make every effort to keep the unity of the Spirit through the bond of peace. In Jesus' name. Amen!

# DISCERNMENT

*"Yes, if you cry out for discernment, And lift up your voice for understanding, If you seek her as silver, and search for her as for hidden treasures; Then you will understand the fear of the Lord, and find the knowledge of God." Proverbs 2:3-5 (NKJV)*

One of my favorite stories is found in *1 Kings 3:16-28* where King Solomon had to use discernment when two harlots came before him, and one wanted him to split the baby in half. Two harlots were pregnant at the same time and lived in the same house. Harlot1 gave birth and harlot2 gave birth three days later. Harlot2 laid on her baby and her baby died, so she waited until harlot1 fell asleep and took harlot1's living baby and replaced it with her dead baby. Harlot1 woke up and examined the dead baby and knew it was not her baby, so both harlots took the matter to King Solomon. Harlot2 wanted King Solomon to split the baby in half and harlot1 told him not to, because she yearned with compassion and wanted him alive, so she asked him to give the living baby to harlot2. Solomon knew then that a real mother would not want her child to be split in half, so he made the right choice based on what he had heard, and gave the living child back to harlot1.

Discernment is very important as well in the workplace. We must examine everything carefully; hold fast to that which is good and abstain from every form of evil.

Paul's prayer for the Church at Philippi in *Philippians 1:9-11: "And this is my prayer: that your love may abound more and more in knowledge and depth of insight, so that you may be able to discern what is best and may be pure and blameless for the day of Christ, filled with the fruit of righteousness that comes through Jesus Christ—to the glory and praise of God. "*

## *Prayer*

Lord, I pray for the spirit of discernment in my life so I will not be engaged in all kinds of unbiblical decision-making and behavior. In Jesus' name. Amen!

# DISCOURAGEMENT
## LET'S TALK

*"Peace I leave with you, My peace I give to you; not as the world gives do I give to you. Let not your heart be troubled, neither let it be afraid." John 14:27*

What is discouragement? Discouragement is a loss of confidence or enthusiasm; dispiritedness.

Have you ever felt discouraged? If your answer is no, please repent right now.

Discouragement is not to be tolerated or pampered. Discouragement must be fought with faith in the Word of God. Lingering in it can cause you to drink, smoke, over-eat, have sleepless nights or even become physically sick.

**TRANSPARENCY ALERT**! I experienced becoming physically sick and experienced sleeplessness because of discouragement and was on medication. What I failed to do back then was to meditate on God's Word, day and night. Instead I rehearsed the situation in my mind day and night. I thank God for my husband and the praying women in my life with whom I was able to be transparent, that prayed me through. Thank You Jesus!

Discouragement can leave you feeling defeated and hopeless and it can suck the very life out of you, if you allow it. Jesus does not want us feeling discouraged. He told us, *"Peace I leave with you, My peace I give to you; not as the world gives do I give to you. Let **not** your heart be troubled, neither let it be afraid." John 14:27.* We must not be moved by what we see or hear in the natural but be moved by what God promises us in His Word. God's Word will NOT return void.

After that workplace episode of discouragement, I vowed to never let anyone in the workplace or out of the workplace cause me to get to that sick place again. To God alone be the glory for great grace during that season.

Let's put on our spiritual armor found in Ephesians 6:14-17, and fight this thing.

# DISCRETION

*"Discretion shall preserve thee, understanding shall keep thee." Proverbs 2:11*

At some point in life, everyone occasionally has said the wrong thing to the wrong person at the wrong time. "Why did I say that?" or "Oh, I just didn't think it through" are common afterthoughts. Another typical reflection after such an awkward situation is "If I had to do it all over again, I would have said this or that. Been there.

Ananias and Sapphira attempted to deceive the Holy Spirit by keeping back part of the price of the land which they had sold, yet saying that they had given all the money to the church. They did not demonstrate discretion by considering what would happen if they lied to God, the All-knowing God who is everywhere at all times and sees everything we do. As a result of their deceit and lack of discretion, they were both struck dead (Acts 5:1-11).

Discretion is applicable in the workplace as well. We have to keep our minds and focus on sound judgment. I am guilty of not always paying attention to what is going on around me and saying the wrong things. In that way, we can better choose our words, attitudes, and actions carefully to model goodness and righteousness for any given situation. When we do that, we avoid words and actions that could result in adverse consequences.

## *Prayer*

Help me Father to regard discretion and that my lips may keep knowledge. Help me to keep sound wisdom and discretion. In Jesus' name. Amen!

## DO UNTO OTHERS

*"And just as you want men to do to you, you also do to them likewise." Luke 6:31 (NKJV)*

Do you remember this "golden rule" growing up? Do unto others as you would like them to do unto you. It was years before I realized it was scriptural. That is a profound command. Think with me for a minute. Can you imagine how well we would all get along? It goes in line with *Matthew 5:7 "Blessed are the merciful for they shall obtain mercy."* Rather than doing to others what they have done to us, sort of like an eye for an eye, or giving them what they may deserve, we are to treat them the way we want them to treat us, regardless.

What if we all put ourselves in other's shoes before we react? What would happen? When we stop for a minute to think how we might like to be treated in a given situation, we build empathy for those actually living that situation. Do you like to be treated with love and respect? Do you like to be treated harsh and mean? When people outright hurt us and are just mean to us all of the time, that is when we really need to pray for them. There is a root to the reason for their actions. It is really deeper than we think. We should feel a level of compassion for those kinds of people. Our responsibility is to pray, regardless.

How are others treating you on your job? How are you treating others on the job? How can you walk in love toward them, regardless?

## *Prayer*

Lord, help me to be mindful of others before I do or say anything. Help me to walk in their shoes so I can do to them, as I would have them do to me. In Jesus' name. Amen!

# ENCOURAGEMENT

*"The LORD is my light and my salvation; whom shall I fear? The LORD is the strength of my life; of whom shall I be afraid." Psalm 27:1*

Throughout the Psalms, we see how David constantly encouraged himself in the Lord. Sometimes, we go through various challenges and no one is around at that particular time to encourage us and suddenly, a song comes to our mind, or a scripture verse. We are left with no one but God. We all need encouragement at some point in our lives. Some need to be encouraged more than others. You might be the one receiving the encouragement all the time or the one giving the encouragement. When we face challenges and go through various tests, a little encouragement goes a long way.

Workplace encouragement is absolutely needed. We all have different jobs. We all have different challenges. Hardship becomes meaningless without encouragement. In I Kings 19:3-10, Elijah the prophet struggled with discouragement. When we are encouraged in the Lord, it gives us the strength to put on our spiritual armor mentioned in Ephesians 6:10-18.

Discouragement is not an uncommon human experience. We may want to give up but we must remember that He who calls us is faithful. Therefore, continue to encourage one another and build each other up, just as you are doing. Encourage each other on the job; no man is an island. Every joint supplies. Let us go the extra mile to build each other up in the workplace.

## *Prayer*

Lord, help me to always have a word of encouragement for others, even if I need encouragement myself. In Jesus' name. Amen!

# PRAYER

I will lift up mine eyes unto the Hills from whence cometh my help. My help cometh from the Lord, Maker of heaven and earth. Hallelujah. Hallelujah. Hallelujah!

I Samuel 12:16 Ever Loving Father, we will stand and see this great thing which the Lord will do before our eyes. Luke 18:27 The things which are impossible with men, we know, are possible with God. Numbers 23:19 Lord, we know too well that God is not a man, that He should lie. Has He said, and will He not do it? James 1:4 But let patience have its perfect work, that we may be perfect and complete, lacking nothing. Romans 8:31 Thank you Lord for reminding us daily, that, If God be for us, who can be against us? 2 Timothy 2:1 We will continue to be strong in the grace that is in Christ Jesus. 2 Timothy 1:13 We will hold fast the pattern of sound words..in faith and love. Colossians 3:2 We will continue to set our minds on things above, not on things on the earth. Colossians 3:23 Lord, whatever we do, we will do it heartily, as to the Lord and not to men. Mark 9:23 If we can believe, all things are possible to him who believes. John 16:33 In the world we will have tribulation; but be of good cheer, we have overcome the world. Hallelujah! Hallelujah. Hallelujah. Hallelujah. Glory!

We are overcomers in Jesus' name. Hallelujah. Hallelujah. Amen!

# EMOTIONS

*"Meekness, temperance: against such there is no law."*
*Galatians 5:23*

It is okay to become emotional, to some extent. God created us emotional, which is why emotions such as love, joy, happiness, guilt, anger, disappointment and fear are revealed in the Scriptures; they are there for us to learn from them. When you are going through an emotional situation, to you, those emotions are powerful and real, but when it comes to the workplace, it is very important that we learn how to manage our emotions, rather than allowing our emotions to manage us.

For example, when we feel upset, it is important to be able to stop, identify what we are upset about, examine our hearts to determine why we are upset, and then proceed in a biblical manner. This is not always easy. Out-of-control emotions tend not to produce God-honoring results: Using the anger emotion, *James 1:20* says *"for the wrath of man does not produce the righteousness of God."*

We know what emotions are operating at the time of operation and we are really still in control. Once recognized, it is up to us to bring them to God, submit to Him and allow Him to do His work in our hearts and direct our actions. Many of the books in Psalms are filled with raw emotions. Sometimes I read them and say, "Oh man, David kept it real." He said whatever he was thinking to God. You have to do the same because God knows your thoughts afar off; therefore it makes no sense to lie to Him. Your mouth might be saying one thing and your heart is saying the truth. Who better to tell the truth? It is okay to share your feelings with the right person. We were not made to go through emotions alone. When we grow in our walk with God, we are able to manage our emotions by being transformed by the renewing of our minds as stated in Romans 12:1–2.

We need daily input of scriptural principles, a desire to grow in the knowledge of God and time spent meditating on God's attributes. We should seek to know more of God, and share more of our hearts with God through prayer. Christian fellowship is another important part of spiritual growth. We journey with fellow believers and help one another grow in faith as well as in emotional maturity.

## *Prayer*

Lord, help me to exercise self-control when dealing with emotions in my everyday affairs in the workplace. In Jesus' name. Amen!

# EXAMINE YOURSELF

*"Examine yourselves, whether ye be in the faith; prove your own selves. Know ye not your own selves, how that Jesus Christ is in you, except ye be reprobates? But I trust that ye shall know that we are not reprobates."*
*II Corinthians 13:5-6*

By the end of this book, you will know just about all of my business. The good thing is, I overcome by the blood of the Lamb and the word of my testimony. There were times when I had to ask myself if I was truly saved based on what I had done or said. If you sincerely go to God with a broken and contrite heart and ask the ever-loving God to show you, you, *He is faithful* to do it.

God showed me, me and I did not like what I saw. I said, the devil is a liar, but with all honesty, the devil was minding his own business. That was not him at all, that was God showing me what I asked Him to show me. It was then my responsibility to accept what He had shown me and repent. Self-examination is part of a continuing process in the life of any Christian who wishes to draw closer to God. We are not here to examine others but to examine ourselves. Our desire should be to not walk around with a form of godliness but denying the power. We must work out our own salvation with fear and trembling.

*Romans 7:14-25 "For we know that the law is spiritual, but I am carnal, sold under sin. For what I am doing, I do not understand. For what I will to do, that I do not practice; but what I hate, that I do. If, then, I do what I will not to do, I agree with the law that it is good. But now, it is no longer I who do it, but sin that dwells in me. For I know that in me (that is, in my flesh) nothing good dwells; for to will is present with me, but how to perform what is good I do not find. For the good that I will to do, I do not do; but the evil I will not to do, that I practice. Now if I do what I will not to do, it is no longer I who do it, but sin that dwells in me. I find then a law, that evil is present with me, the one who wills to do good. For I delight in the law of God according to the inward man. But I see another law in my members, warring against the law of my mind, and bringing me into captivity to the law of sin which is in my members. O wretched man that I am! Who will deliver me from this body of death? I thank God— through Jesus Christ our Lord! So then, with the mind I myself serve the law of God, but with the flesh the law of sin."*

## *Prayer*

Lord, help me to honestly examine myself daily and to rely on You to show me what is displeasing in your sight. In Jesus' name. Amen!

# FAITH

*"And Jesus answering saith unto them, Have faith in God." Mark 11:22*

There are several stories in the bible of different people exercising faith and seeing its manifestations. I will focus my attention on the story of the woman with the issue of blood. That story is dear to me because of some health challenges I experienced for several months in 2014 and the early part of 2015. Her accounts are found in *Matthew 9:20-22, Mark 5:24-34 and Luke 8:43-48* ................ And He said to her, "Daughter, be of good cheer; your faith has made you well. Go in peace." Please read the different accounts when you have the chance. The blessing now is, you and I don't have to press through a crowd to reach Jesus like this woman did. Just have faith in Jesus Christ and Him crucified and His finished work at the Cross.

Our faith just needs to be present. Jesus encourages his disciples that even a little faith will go a long way. Sometimes we have situations that seem impossible, but the truth of the matter is, nothing is impossible with God. There are people somewhere relying on their faith in God for something to eat, because they have nothing. Some are relying on their faith in God for healing manifestations, provision and protection.

It could be that you have faith to believe that your work day is going to be productive and you just need to make it through the day, or that your rent/mortgage is due and you are believing for provision.

What are you believing God for today? *Hebrews 11:1 "Now faith is the substance of things hoped for, the evidence of things not seen."*

## *Prayer*

Lord, help me to walk by faith and not by sight. In Jesus' name. Amen!

# FEAR

*"Fear thou not; for I am with thee: be not dismayed; for I am thy God: I will strengthen thee; yea, I will help thee; yea, I will uphold thee with the right hand of my righteousness." Isaiah 41:10*

Years ago, I worked at a firm in Connecticut. I remember it like it was yesterday. I made a mistake on a file. This was a financial mistake. When I recognized the mistake, I was like, oh my, I am a goner. Another secretary called me to ask what happened and said "someone called to speak to that attorney and I transferred the call to him." Fear gripped my heart. I was very grateful for the heads-up because I knew once he was off the phone, he would have called me in his office. I felt fear deep within my gut. When he got off the phone, he did not call me. He came straight to me. I saw him coming from the other end of the hallway and he saw me go under my desk. Now picture this: a grown woman hiding under a desk. I heard him say, "Charleen." I answered, "She is not here." He said, "come from under that desk." Then he asked in his calm voice, "what happened?" I explained and I got a good gentle talking to. When I reflect on that moment, I ask myself, why in the world did I go under the desk? Only two things could have happened that day. He had a choice to fire me or keep me. He kept me and I worked with him until I resigned, years later.

*"There is no fear in love; but perfect love casts out fear, because fear involves torment. But he who fears has not been made perfect in love." I John 4:18*

Why do we become fearful? We become fearful when we expect punishment because we know we've done something wrong. In our relationship with God, the devil will always try to point us to ourselves — point us to our shortcomings, failures and sins. Once we start beholding ourselves in our sins, instead of Christ (our new identity) in all His glory, we start expecting God to punish us. There is something within us that knows God is holy, and when we compare His perfect holiness to our sins, we think He wants to punish us. However, Jesus Christ bore all of our sins, and the punishment they called for, in His very own body on the Cross. Now that we are in Christ, we are righteous, holy and blameless. Hallelujah.

Whatever you may be fearful of today — instead of trying to uproot the fear, uproot any condemnation that you may be experiencing, and with it, the fear will go away. Know that God will never punish you, because He punished Jesus in your place. You are God's beloved, righteous child whom He wants to bless abundantly!

## *Prayer*

Lord, when fear grips my heart, bring to my remembrance that you have not given me the spirit of fear; but of power, and of love, and of a sound mind, and that perfect love casts out fear. In Jesus' name. Amen!

# FORGIVE

*"For if you forgive men their trespasses, your heavenly Father will also forgive you. But if you do not forgive men their trespasses, neither will your Father forgive your trespasses." Matthew 6:14-15 (NKJV)*

This topic is really dear to my heart. We can all testify to this fact that we have wrestled with unforgiveness and wrestled with asking others to forgive us. I have gone through a particular season of unforgiveness. That season of my life, I just felt like the most mis-understood person alive, because I was going through stuff that just caused me to separate myself and landed myself in an unselfish place called me, myself and I. That place felt good. God loves me so much, and He loves you too, that he started showing me, me, a little at a time. I had no choice but to repent and get some things right.

I was offending people left, right, back and center without even realizing it. Now, I feel like I have mastered the art of asking, "please forgive me" and saying "I am truly sorry." To whom much is given, much is required. God is such an example. There are just so many reasons to not forgive, in our sight, but unforgiveness is a wicked thing. The truth is, unlimited forgiveness must be demonstrated with mercy toward others, because it is the reflection of a right relationship with God. God's forgiveness of our sins should motivate us to forgive those who offend us. Do you have a right relationship with God?

## *Prayer*

Lord, remind me that whenever I stand praying to forgive, if I have anything against anyone, so that my Father who is in heaven will also forgive me my transgressions. But if I do not forgive, neither will my Father who is in heaven forgive my transgressions. In Jesus' name. Amen!

## FORGIVENESS-CHALLENGE

*"And be ye kind one to another, tenderhearted, forgiving one another, even as God for Christ's sake hath forgiven you." Ephesians 4:32*

## *Truth Moment between you and God*

We have ALL been hurt, offended, gossiped about, betrayed, etc. But when you think about it, we have, at some point, does those same things to others.

List 10 things you have done, in the past or even now, to require forgiveness. How did it make you feel when you were forgiven?

1. _____

2. _____

3. _____

4. _____

5. _____

6. _____

7. _____

8. _____

9. _____

10. _____

List 10 people you find it really hard to forgive and go to God and ask Him to help you forgive.

1. _____

2. _____

3. _____

4. _____

5. _____

6. _____

7. _____

8. _____

9. _____

10. _____

## *Prayer*

Lord, help me to forgive quickly. In Jesus' name. Amen!

# GOD FIGHTS FOR YOU

*"I will go before thee, and make the crooked places straight: I will break in pieces the gates of brass, and cut in sunder the bars of iron." Isaiah 45:2*

Situations come about from time to time where we might feel the need to defend ourselves and take matters into our own hands-"I will show him or her." Well, with God, that is not the case. God tells us to not go out with haste, nor go by flight; for He will go before us, and the God of Israel will be our rear-guard. He also said He will fight for us, and we shall hold our peace because He will contends with him who contend with us. Now, how cool is that? Knowing that we don't have to fight any battles because there is one who will fight for us. He is our Defender. We are soldiers in the

Lord's army and our weapons are the Word, prayer and faith in any given situation. All we need to do is to stand and see the great things the Lord will do before our eyes. He is an awesome God and He does fight our battles for us.

What battle are you facing on the job? How does knowing God fights your battles for you make you feel?

## *Prayer*

Lord, remind me that the battles I fight are not for me to fight, it is for me to trust You and to stand still and see the great thing You will do before my eyes. In Jesus' name. Amen!

# GOSSIP

*"A talebearer revealeth secrets: but he that is of a faithful spirit concealeth the matter." Proverbs 11:13*

What is the meaning of gossip?

1. To spread secrets or rumors - Proverbs 11:13; 20:19.

2. Slander

3. To reveal personal facts about another

I know you readers never struggle in this area. Guess what? I have from time to time. I am seriously working on this. Sometimes we categorize gossip as little gossip and big gossip, but it is one in the same. Someone does us wrong, and we gossip about it. We might hear something and we talk about it to someone else. It has absolutely nothing to do with you or the person involved, so why talk about it?

We gossip at the coffee machine, on the phone, at the copy machine, in our office, by text and email. It is so easy to get caught up in gossip. The reality is, gossip can cause lack of trust and morale, can cause the hearer to quit his/her job, can cause division, can cause hurt feelings and cause the workplace to be unhealthy. We know what gossip can do in the workplace. Let us purpose in our hearts to just do what God wants us to do, and not partake in gossip. We are called to shun the appearance of evil.

*"Abstain from all appearance of evil. And the very God of peace sanctify you wholly; and I pray God your whole spirit and soul and body be preserved blameless unto the coming of our Lord Jesus Christ. Faithful is he that calleth you, who also will do it." I Thessalonians 5:22-24*

## *Prayer*

LORD please keep my tongue from saying evil things and my lips from speaking deceitful things. Set a guard, O LORD, over my mouth; Keep watch over the door of my lips. My lips shall not speak wickedness, nor my tongue utter deceit because a perverse man stirs up dissension, and a gossip separates close friends. Lord, help me to not be a gossip. Remind me Lord, that a man or woman who lacks judgment derides his neighbor, but a man of understanding holds his tongue. A gossip betrays a confidence, but a trustworthy man keeps a secret. The words of a gossip are like choice morsels; they go down to a man's inmost parts. Lord, help me today and always to let no unwholesome word proceed from my mouth, but only such a word as is good for edification according to the need of the moment, so that it will give grace to those who hear. In Jesus' name. Amen!

# GOSSIP-CHALLENGE

*"Whoso keepeth his mouth and his tongue keepeth his soul from troubles." Proverbs 21:23*

There are no such things as big gossip and little gossip. Just like sin is sin, gossip is gossip.

What are some reasons why you gossip?

1. _____

2. _____

3. _____

4. _____

5. _____

How did it make you feel when you knew someone gossiped about you? What kind of emotions did you experience?

1. _____

2. _____

3. _____

4. _____

5. _____

**I am challenging you to do the following:**

1. To not say anything negative about anyone in or outside the workplace for 5 days, then increase it to 10, 15, 20, 25, 30 days. If at first you don't succeed, try, try, try again.

2. If someone does something to you, talk to God about it. Do not mention it to others and get them involved, not even your spouse.

3.  If someone is talking to you about someone in the workplace, do not join forces and say yeah or nay.

4.  Encourage the one talking about the situation in a positive way.

5.  Change the subject.

## *Prayer*

Father God in the name of Jesus, help me to bridle my tongue daily because a fool utters his mind, but a wise man keeps it in. In Jesus' name. Amen!

# GRATITUDE
# LET'S TALK

*"In everything give thanks; for this is the will of God in Christ Jesus for you." I Thessalonians 5:18*

Please get a sheet of paper, ipad, cell phone, etc. Add numbers 1 through 30 going down the left (example below) and answer this question. You might be able to come up with your list of 30 things in 10 minutes, or it could possibly take you all day, a week, even a month. Oh, by the way, if you are led, please feel free to *not* stop at 30, but continue on.

List 30 or more things you are grateful for in the workplace.

1. _____

2. _____

3. _____

4. _____

Now that you have completed your list of the 30 or more things you are grateful for in the workplace, how does that make you feel right now? Pause for a minute. What emotion/emotions are you experiencing?

Side Note: In 2015, during my complaining, when the Lord dropped this list into my spirit, I was like wow! Truth be told, I had *never* before made a list such as this one. Have you? I have made grocery lists, lists of things I am believing God for, to-do lists, vision lists and lists of things I would like to do before I depart this life, etc.

We fall into the trap of complaining from time to time....well not you, but me, because I know you NEVER complain, so I will talk about myself right here.

**TRANSPARENCY ALERT**! I fall into the trap of complaining from time to time, forgetting how grateful I should always be. God said "in *everything*," not in some things, to give thanks. I have come a long way in the complaining department, but I have not yet arrived at my destination of absolutely no complaining. For me this is a journey. I have employed the work of the Holy Spirit to get me there, because there is no way on earth I can get there on my own. Because the Holy Spirit is now involved, this is the reason why I am *"being confident of this very thing, that He which hath begun a good work in me, will perform it until the day of Jesus Christ." Philippians 1:6.*

Complaining might not be an area of weakness for you. Giving thanks might be your greatest strength. If we are completely honest with ourselves, we can start our own *list*-there goes that word again-our own list of weaknesses and ask God to help us in those areas. Where you fall short, you should be just as confident of God's Philippians 1:6 promise.

After you have completed your list, keep it and just go back to it from time to time. Trust me, when the urge to complain comes to your mind, all or some of the things you wrote on your list will come back to your memory. There are times you might ignore the urge and complain (been there), but when you later reflect, you will prayerfully be convicted and ask God to forgive you. It is at that point you will recognize how grateful you truly are. Please join me in faithful gratitude for employers.

# HUMBLE

*"Humble yourselves therefore under the mighty hand of God, that he may exalt you in due time." I Peter 5:6*

Being humble is a sure cure for pride. I am telling you this from experience. Am I always humble? No, not all the time, but I know when I am getting prideful. The Spirit in me convicts me. When we are humble, we submit to God and we repent. True humility is holding low esteem or opinion of our own goodness and always ready to give God the glory. We must abase ourselves because we realize our sinfulness, and, therefore, we are willing to depend on God to meet our needs.

When we know we cannot truly succeed in our own strength, that is being humble. It is thanking

God for our talents and gifts, and giving him credit for our accomplishments. Humility is seeking to build others up, _not ourselves_. It is walking in God's love, forgiveness and grace.

Our attitude should be the same as that of Christ Jesu*s*. When we are humble, we can respond to and learn from criticism without becoming defensive—whether it is deserved or not deserved. When we are humble, we apologize. We can develop a humble spirit by being mindful not to take credit for anything, but to always acknowledge God as the one who made it possible.

Let us take a good look at our "humble" chart and ask God to help us to locate where we are on that chart and go from there. He is doing a new thing, it shall spring forth and we will know it.

## _Prayer_

Lord, help me to walk in humility because when pride comes, then comes disgrace, but with humility comes wisdom. Help me to not fall into the trap of pride, but to walk in humility towards Jehovah, all the time. In Jesus' name. Amen!

# HUMILITY

*"Do nothing from selfish ambition or conceit, but in humility count others more significant than yourselves. Let each of you look not only to his own interests, but also to the interests of others."*
*Philippians 2:3-4 (NKJV)*

What is true humility? According to *2 Corinthians 5:15,* when someone is humble they are focused on God and others, not self. Their focus on others is out of a desire to love and glorify God.... A humble person's goal is to elevate God and encourage others. In short, they no longer live for themselves, but for Him who died on the Cross and rose again on their behalf.

I truly had to examine myself also in this area. I really do not want to have a form of Godliness and deny the power therein. I can honestly say, I have not fully arrived in this area. God loves us so much that he gives us opportunities daily to exercise humility in the workplace.

I must decrease so God can increase.

## *Prayer*

Jesus, help me to walk in a manner worthy of the calling to which I have been called, with all humility and gentleness, with patience, bearing with one another in love, eager to maintain the unity of the Spirit in the bond of peace. In Jesus' name. Amen!

# HUMILITY
# LET'S TALK

*"Let nothing be done through strife or vainglory; but in lowliness of mind let each esteem other better than themselves. Look not every man on his own things, but every man also on the things of others." Philippians 2:3-4*

"Humility isn't about thinking less of yourself," as the British writer C.S. Lewis once put it, "but thinking of yourself less." A humble person will defer glory and credit to God, not boasting in his/her own self.

Why are we not humble people? I am glad you asked. My answer is, we are not humble because we want to get the glory for ourselves, for our achievements and our accomplishments. The **real** reason is, there is a war going on inside of us. Every single day, our flesh wrestles against our spirit. Brother Paul, in Galatians 5:17, says it better: "*For the flesh lusteth against the Spirit, and the Spirit against the flesh: and these are contrary the one to the other: so that ye cannot do the things that ye would.*" A sure way to practice humility is by acknowledging God as the source of all that is good, and knowing we could not do or achieve things on our own. Being consistently thankful, and acknowledging God and His daily grace in every area of our life is the central part of Christian humility.

**TRANSPARENCY ALERT**! What I am learning is, it is not what we say but how we say it. I can get excited about something and when I share all the excitement, it can come across as being haughty or arrogant. These days I am mindful of what to share and how to share it, making sure I acknowledge God and give Him the glory. The latter part of 2015 to early 2016, I went through a situation that caused me to humble myself under the mighty hands of God. Did I like it? Absolutely not, but I knew for sure that everything I went through was working together for my good. The blessing in that situation was knowing that I was not alone, His grace was sufficient to keep me, and that situation would pass. Know what I mean?

What have you experienced, or probably are experiencing now, that has brought you to a place of humility? We can all use a slice of "humble pie" every now and then. Don't you agree?

# INTEGRITY

*"The integrity of the upright shall guide them: but the perverseness of transgressors shall destroy them." Proverbs 11:3*

*"Then this Daniel distinguished himself above the governors and satraps, because an excellent spirit was in him; and the king gave thought to setting him over the whole realm." Daniel 6:3*

Where does integrity starts? It start in the heart. Keep thy heart with all diligence; for out of it are the issues of life. People of integrity keep their word, their yes is yes and their no is no. Daniel was genuine, he was honest, he was righteous through and through. He was consistent in his personal life and in his professional life. Men even hired spies to watch Daniel for days on end, to see if they could catch him in any breach of his integrity. Integrity is living a life every day, knowing that God is there with us, looking at us 24 hours a day, whether anybody else is there or not. The spies reported, "there's nothing there and the only way you're ever going to trap this man is if you can find some way to trap him on the basis of his faith." So they set up a trap. See how easy we can start mess? They went to Darius the king and they tickled his ears [flattered him]. They said, "Darius, we want to make you a god for a month." Darius liked that idea. Ego kicked in right away. Therefore, for the next 30 days, the only way anybody could pray, was to pray to Darius.

*"Now when Daniel learned that the decree had been published, he went home to his upstairs room where the windows opened toward Jerusalem. Three times a day he got down on his knees and prayed, giving thanks to his God, just as he had done before." Daniel 6:10.*

Daniel was not fearful of the decree; he knew the God he served. Daniel was caught in the trap and they threw Daniel into the lion's den. That is a great story, because it is the story of a man who kept his integrity. That's integrity that begins in the heart.

## *Prayer*

Lord, You give wisdom; from Your mouth come knowledge and understanding; You store up sound wisdom for the upright; You are a shield to those who walk in integrity, guarding the paths of justice and watching over the way of Your saints. Help me to walk in integrity daily. In Jesus' name. Amen!

# JOB SECURITY

*"It is better to trust in the Lord than to put confidence in man." Psalm 118:8*

I stop by to remind us that in this life here on earth, there is no such thing as job security. We must never put our trust in our job. Anything can go wrong and the rug can be pulled from under our feet. The only sure security we have in this life is Jesus. He cannot lie. He is the same yesterday, today and forever. God is our sure Foundation. This Rock is Jesus.

We have to be mindful not to think we are safe on our job. Sometimes all it takes is one or two bad decisions to cause a company to fall. Job loss can cause some to go into deep depression, commit suicide or turn to drugs and alcohol instead of turning to Jesus, who is our Source, Provider and our Strength.

One of my favorite songs:*

*"My hope is built on nothing less than Jesus' blood and righteousness. I dare not trust the sweetest frame, but wholly lean on Jesus' name. **Refrain**: On Christ the solid rock I stand, __all__ other ground is sinking sand; __all__ other ground is sinking sand"*

A clue: "all" other. So that song is saying to me that everything and everyone outside of Jesus is sinking sand.

Examine where you are in the workplace and if you feel that your trust is in your employer, repent and ask God to forgive you.

## *Prayer*

Lord, remind me daily that on Christ the Solid Rock I stand and that all other ground is sinking sand. In Jesus' name. Amen!

*\*My Hope Is Built on Nothing Less, by Edward Mote (Public Domain)*

# KINDNESS

*"And be ye kind one to another, tenderhearted, forgiving one another, even as God for Christ's sake hath forgiven you." Ephesians 4:32*

Joseph is my example of the verse above. Here is a quick run-down. Please read Genesis chapters 37-50 for the full account. Joseph was the son of Jacob's old age with the woman he loved with all his heart, Rachel. Joseph was favored more than his brothers. His brothers knew it and they did not like him. His brothers threw him in a pit one day, he was sold into slavery, lied on by Potipher's wife because he rejected her, thrown in the prison and later given all power in Egypt. See, Joseph was a dreamer. He always had dreams but never knew what they meant until he was older, and the Lord started revealing his dreams to him.

Years later, there was a famine in the land, so his brothers traveled to Egypt to get grain. Joseph recognized his brothers, but they did not recognize him. Can you just put yourself in Joseph's shoes for a minute? What would you have done if that happened to you? He wept when he saw them. Joseph, out of the kindness of his heart, because he had a heart for God, forgave them and made sure they got lots of grain. He also moved them to Egypt to stay with him. He showed kindness to everyone in his family.

If we have a heart for God, it is easy for us to be kind to others. This would have been me, in my carnal state: "Oh no they didn't, they did me wrong, they ain't getting nothing. I'm gonna show them." In my carnal state, I would have reminded them of what they did. Thank God I am moving on to deeper depth in God.

Kindness should be contagious. Does it hurt you to be kind to someone?

## *Prayer*

Lord, help me to show kindness to everyone I come in contact with. In Jesus' name. Amen!

## KINDNESS-CHALLENGE

*"Do not let kindness and truth leave you; Bind them around your neck, Write them on the tablet of your heart." Proverbs 3:3 (NJKV)*

Just do something nice.

1. Hold the elevator.

2. If someone is in the elevator with you or even the lobby, give that person a compliment.

3. If you go out to lunch, just look for someone to compliment.

4. If you are out during lunch and walk by a car with an expired meter, feed the meter.

5. Offer a smile.

6. Take the time to hand-write a letter/note to someone you know is having some challenges and encourage him/her.

7. Show empathy.

## *Prayer*

Lord, help me to show kindness to everyone I come in contact with. In Jesus' name. Amen!

# LAZINESS

*"For even when we were with you, we commanded you this: If anyone will not work, neither shall he eat."*
*2 Thessalonians 3:10 (NJKV)*

Can we expect to *not* work and get paid?

Matthew 25 talks about how a man travelling to a far country gave his servants "talents" – a type of money in those days. The one who was given five talents invested them and gained five more. The one given two talents also invested them and gained two more. However, the one given only one talent dug a hole in the ground and hid it in the ground. Listen to the weird excuse in verses 24-25: *"Then he which had received the one talent came and said, Lord, I knew thee that thou art an hard man, reaping where thou hast not sown, and gathering where thou hast not strawed: And I was afraid, and went and hid thy talent [money] in the earth: lo, there thou hast that is thine."*

Now, if he knew that his master would dig up the earth like that, then the worst place to put the money was in the ground! His master said to him in vs 26 *"But his lord answered and said to him, 'You wicked and lazy servant, you knew that I reap where I have not sown, and gather where I have not scattered seed."*

## *Prayer*

Father God, in the name of Jesus, I bind up the spirit of laziness far from me. May the works of my hands bring favor and great fulfillment. Open my eyes to see and do what you would have me do. Help me to perform my duties with joy and gratitude. I am reminded in *Hebrews 6:12 "We do not want you to become lazy, but to imitate those who through faith and patience inherit what has been promised.*"

# LIGHT

*"Let your light so shine before men, that they may see your good works, and glorify your Father which is in heaven." Matthew 5:16*

Sing with me:*

"This little light of mine

I'm gonna let it shine

This little light of mine

I'm gonna let it shine

This little light of mine

I'm gonna let it shine

Let it shine, let it shine, let it shine"

I am fixing to have church up in here. Amen! I think the majority of us grew up with this song in Sunday school, remember? When I think of the word "shine", what comes to mind are a diamond ring, my kitchen floor after it has been polished, and my car after it has been waxed. You have your list too. The diamond ring and the kitchen floor can become dull after a while if they are not cleaned and polished. The same with us. If we become intoxicated with sin and the cares of this world, our light will quickly grow dim and go out. We have the greatest opportunity to exemplify Christ in the workplace. Jesus is the Light and as Christ is, so are we in the earth.

One night around 11:30 pm-ish, I turned off all the lights in the house and turned on a pen light and sat it on the night stand. I walked to the door and looked at the light and was able to see where that light was. Because I was able to see the light on the other side of the room, I was able to walk right to it. Right there in that moment, the Holy Spirit revealed to me that I don't have to worry about being a lamp or a flood light, that I just need to shine. Because I was able to walk to that light, people will walk to me as they see me shine. I realized how small that light was; it was tiny, but it was shining. That is all He asks of us in the workplace. Our light shines when we act out the word daily. People will form an opinion about what they think based on how you act. Our light must shine.

I believe by the spirit, God is getting ready to do something "big" in our lives. He is going to catapult us to the next level. We must believe it in order to receive it.

## Prayer

Lord, help me to light up the workplace by my speech and my actions.

*This Little Light Of Mine by Harry Dixon Loes (Public Domain)*

# LOVE

*"But I say unto you, Love your enemies, bless them that curse you, do good to them that hate you, and pray for them which despitefully use you, and persecute you." Matthew 5:44*

The three Greek words for love are Agape, Eros and Phileo. Eros is erotic love between lovers and Phileo is the love between friends. My focus is on Agape love.

*Agape Love* - It is the most self-sacrificing love that there is. This type of love is the love that God has for His children. This type of love is what was displayed on the cross by Jesus Christ.

*Agape Love* is the God kind of love that we should have for everyone we encounter. For God so loved the **world**, not just you. I am going to draw from a few verses read at my wedding. *I Corinthians 13:4-8 "Love suffers long and is kind; love does not envy; love does not parade itself, is not puffed up; does not behave rudely, does not seek its own, is not provoked, thinks no evil; does not rejoice in iniquity, but rejoices in the truth; bears all things, believes all things, hopes all things, endures all things. Love never fails."* Agape love is that unconditional love, no matter what and in spite of. I am going to ask you to just meditate on those verses and let them get deep down into your spirit.

I don't know about you, but I am working on my love walk daily. Some days seem harder than others. We don't get to choose who to love and who not to love. It does not matter what others have done to us. Love forgives. Repetition is the best teacher, so here you go. *I Corinthians 13:4-8 "Love suffers long and is kind; love does not envy; love does not parade itself, is not puffed up; does not behave rudely, does not seek its own, is not provoked, thinks no evil; does not rejoice in iniquity, but rejoices in the truth; bears all things, believes all things, hopes all things, endures all things. Love never fails.*" We are commanded to walk in the God kind of love towards everyone we encounter daily. This love just does not happen overnight. It has to be a deep desire and be developed with the help of the Holy Spirit. To do so, we must get to know God through daily meditating on His Word. He is the Word. He is Love.

## *Prayer*

Lord, because the love of God is shed abroad in my heart by the Holy Spirit, You will help me to love others from a true heart. In Jesus' name. Amen!

# MOTIVE

*"Every way of a man [is] right in his own eyes: but the LORD pondereth the hearts." Proverbs 21:2*

What is motive? Motive is a reason for doing something, especially one that is *hidden* or not obvious.

Why is it so important to have the right motive when we are doing something? Because it pleases God, and the wrong motives can easily backfire. We reap what we sow is a biblical law. Before we attempt to do something we must examine ourselves. We can do the right things to impress others only to make ourselves look good. We have to be so careful not to chase after our own glory, whether it involves ministry, family or the workplace.

Have you ever been asked to do something and you asked, what's in it for me? Think about it: why does something have to be in it for you? Whatever we do, we are commanded to do it as unto the Lord. God wants us to perform from a true heart. When we have the right motive, we are allowing God to work on our behalf. We are allowing Him to move in our direction. There is joy in a true heart that functions on pure motives.

I have heard, and you probably have too, of many workplace horror stories, about things that others have done just to get ahead. Let every man examine himself.

## *Prayer*

Lord, help me to examine my motives before I do or commit to anything, making sure it will glorify You and not me. In Jesus' name. Amen!

# MURMURING

*"Do all things without murmurings and disputings."*
*Philippians 2:14*

Some years ago, during my unemployment, Arthur and I were going through some financial challenges in our marriage and some back to back emergencies. When the challenges started, he gave me a good lecture about how not to murmur or complain but to trust God for our situation. I did not view it as murmuring and complaining. I simply viewed it as talking about it. He then went on to explain that was the reason the children of God were in the wilderness for so long. I thought to myself, oh Lord, here we go. I honestly thought his pride was the reason why he did not want me to talk about those challenges we were having. But the truth of the matter is, he was absolutely right. Murmuring shows a lack of faith and that we don't trust God. But it feels so good to complain. That was quite challenging for me, the talker in our relationship.

At that time, family and friends would ask, how are you guys doing and I would say, oh, we are doing great on this end. One day my dad called and said, so what is going on down there, how is the job search? It was at the tip of my tongue to say, daddy we need $$$. Can you deposit some $$$ into our account? My dad is the go-to man, bless his heart. He would not have said no to me. He would say, "let me talk to Dee Dee (mom) and get back to you," and mommy would have said "yes." I kept hearing Arthur's voice in my head saying "we must trust God for our situation." That was where we had to just rely solely on God and wait for Him to show up. He divinely showed up and got us back on track, before I started working. He alone got the glory.

If you have NEVER had financial challenges, I want you to lift your hands up right now and just give God some praise, glory and honor. I just praised Him with you.

Sometimes we encounter situations on the job that we feel the need to murmur and complain about. But the truth is, we really don't have to murmur about stuff. Pray instead and watch God move.

## *Prayer*

Lord, I ask You to help me to not murmur or complain about my job, but to be thankful always because it is Your will concerning me. In Jesus' name. Amen!

# MURMURING-CHALLENGE

*"These are murmurers, complainers, walking after their own lusts; and their mouth speaketh great swelling words, having men's persons in admiration because of advantage." Jude 1:16*

What are some things you murmur about?

1. _____

2. _____

3. _____

4. _____

5. _____

6. _____

7. _____

8. _____

What actions can you take now to stop murmuring?

1. _____

2. _____

3. _____

4. _____

5. _____

6. _____

7. _____

8. _____

## *Prayer*

Lord, before I open my mouth to start murmuring, remind me that when I murmur I am saying I do not trust You. In Jesus' name. Amen!

## OBEDIENCE
## BLESSINGS ON OBEDIENCE

*Deuteronomy 28: 1-8*

*"Now it shall come to pass, if you diligently obey the voice of the Lord your God, to observe carefully all His commandments which I command you today, that the Lord your God will set you high above all nations of the earth. And all these blessings shall come upon you and overtake you, because you obey the voice of the Lord your God: Blessed shall you be in the city, and blessed shall you be in the country. Blessed shall be the fruit of your body, the produce of your ground and the increase of your herds, the increase of your cattle and the offspring of your flocks. Blessed shall be your basket and your kneading bowl. Blessed shall you be when you come in, and blessed shall you be when you go out.*

*The Lord will cause your enemies who rise against you to be defeated before your face; they shall come out against you one way and flee before you seven ways."*

## Prayer

Lord, help me to diligently obey Your voice, to observe carefully all Your commandments which You command me today, that the Lord my God will set me high above all nations of the earth, and all these blessings shall come upon me and overtake me, because I obey the voice of the Lord my God. In Jesus' name. Amen!

# OFFENSE

*"A brother offended is harder to be won than a strong city: and their contentions are like the bars of a castle."*
*Proverbs 18:19*

Are you easily offended? We get offended if someone looks at us the wrong way or someone says something we don't like. There are so many ways we get offended and ways we have also offended others. I highly recommend the book "The Bait of Satan" by John Bevere. He mentioned that offense is one of the snares Satan uses to get us out of the will of God. I read his book some years ago and I think I need to re-visit it. We are sometimes too sensitive. My mom said to me some years ago, get over it, you are too "thin skinned". I was more offended when she said that, like, no she didn't. As I grew in grace, I realized that when we are "thin skinned," as mom puts it, we are not seasoned enough. As I mature in Christ, I realize when we are easily offended, we have not yet died to self, and self cannot please God.

Paul said it best in *Galatians 2:20 "I have been crucified with Christ; it is no longer I who live, but Christ lives in me."* Jesus taught that this is the way of the Christian life, that if anyone wants to follow Him, they must "take up their cross daily" (Luke 9:23). We must become totally immersed in the identity and person of Jesus Christ, dying to self and allowing Christ to live through us, so that when offenses come, we see the offender in love and forgive them. Help me Holy Ghost.

Are you easily offended in work-related situations? David said in *Psalm 119:11 "I have hidden your word in my heart that I might not sin against you"* and to take an offense is to sin against God.

The blessing in taking an offense is, the Lord will speak to us, if we are sensitive to His still small voice.

## *Prayer*

Lord, help me daily to not be offended in situations but to always remember that I am crucified with Christ and it is no longer I who live but Christ who lives in me. In Jesus' name. Amen!

# PATIENCE

*"Now we exhort you, brethren, warn them that are unruly, comfort the feebleminded, support the weak, be patient toward all men." I Thessalonians 5:14*

I have been getting quite a bit of practice in this area. Whenever I feel like I don't want to exercise patience with someone, the Lord quickly reminds me that to whom much is given, much is required. We can easily develop a spirit of impatience which leads to stress, anger and frustration, because we forget where we are coming from. We had to, at some point, learn what we now know to get us to where we are. I can honestly make a long list of employers, office managers and co-workers-well, maybe the list is not that long ☺ - who had to exercise patience with me because stuff was not clicking.

There are many situations at work that can cause us to lose our patience with each other. If we take a look at our average workday, we will find many occasions where we can lose our patience. Losing patience causes anger and unhappiness and harms relationships. This might also make us say and do things that we would regret later.

What we must realize is that we cannot change people, but we can change our reaction to them. We can learn to choose how we react. We can wait a little while before reacting. We may not be able to change our reaction the first time we try, but if we try over and over again, sooner or later, we will have more control over our reactions.

## *Prayer*

Lord, You are the perfect example of patience. As You are patient with me, help me to be patient with others. In Jesus' name. Amen!

# PEACE
## LET'S TALK

"Peace I leave with you, My peace I give to you; not as the world gives do I give to you. Let not your heart be troubled, neither let it be afraid." John 14:27

Peace is the *third* portion of the fruit of the Spirit mentioned in Galatians 5:22-23. Do you yearn for peace? Why don't you have it? A sure way to know if you have the peace of God ruling in your heart and mind is your reaction to situations.

**TRANSPARENCY ALERT**: July 28, 2016, I woke up so happy and excited and just praising God for who He is in my life. I was having such a great morning until a few hours later, when I received information that really got me all bent out of shape. Yes, bent out of shape. I was NOT sober and vigilant and was caught off guard. I got anxious and kept saying Lord have mercy, Jesus. My flesh got the best of me. I reacted quickly instead of adhering to *Philippians 4:6 "Be anxious for nothing, but in everything by prayer and supplication, with thanksgiving, let your requests be made known to God; and the peace of God, which surpasses all understanding, will guard your hearts and minds through Christ Jesus."*

I made a phone call and left a message. I did not wait for my call to be returned. I started sending emails and cc'd the different parties that were involved. When I got my phone call returned, we talked and I was still anxious. I was told it would take a week before the changes took effect. In the follow-up email, the company apologized and agreed to reimburse me $$$$. I was not expecting reimbursement; I just wanted the problem to be fixed immediately. I thanked God for that unexpected reimbursement.

That situation robbed me of my peace for about three hours or so. I sent a couple of emails/text messages to three of my prayer partners and they prayed and encouraged me in the situation. Later I reflected on what had transpired and I thought, Charleen, God's peace was not ruling your heart and mind. I had to have a talk with myself. I spoke to the Lord, repented and asked Him to forgive me.

The first thing I should have done was talk to God. I should have acknowledged Him in all my ways so He could direct my path. Do you find yourself getting bent out of shape over situations? We really have to make a conscious effort to not let situations and people rob us of our peace, and get all bent out of shape like I did. I am going to ask you to do something. The next time the peace stealer comes, or you can sense him coming, pause before you react and PRAY. Talk to God before you react and see what happens.

# PERSECUTION

*"Blessed are ye, when men shall revile you, and persecute you, and shall say all manner of evil against you falsely, for my sake. Rejoice, and be exceeding glad: for great is your reward in heaven: for so persecuted they the prophets which were before you."*
*Matthew 5:11-12*

This is what Paul said in *I Corinthians 15:9-10 "For I am the least of the apostles, who am not worthy to be called an apostle, because I **persecuted** the church of God. But by the grace of God I am what I am, and His grace toward me was not in vain; but I labored more abundantly than they all, yet not I, but the grace of God which was with me."*

Have you persecuted anyone with your tongue lately? Have you ever been persecuted? Pray for the one who is persecuting you, and ask God for grace and patience to go through it. Examine yourself to see if you have persecuted or are currently persecuting anyone, and ask for forgiveness.

## *Prayer*

Lord, help me to persevere under trials; for once I have been approved, I will receive the crown of life which the Lord has promised to those who love Him. In Jesus' name. Amen!

# PRAYER

Hallelujah. Hallelujah. Glory! Thank You Jesus. Hallelujah. Hallelujah. Worshipful Father, I bless, honor, praise and thank You. Hallelujah. Hallelujah! Thank you for your promises, Holy One.

And our God will meet all our needs according to his glorious riches in Christ Jesus (*Philippians4:1*). You told us, do not worry about our lives, what we will eat or drink; or about our bodies, what we will wear. You asked us, is not life more important than food, and the body more important than clothes? You asked us to look at the birds of the air because they do not sow or reap or store away in barns, and yet You, our heavenly Father, feed them. Are we not much more valuable than they? (*Matthew*

*6:25-26).* Thank you for reminding us daily to seek first your kingdom and your righteousness, and all these things will be given to us as well (*Matthew 6:31-33*). Lord, we fully obey You, our God, and today carefully follow all your commands you gave because You will set us high above all the nations of the earth; you will grant us abundant prosperity in the fruit of our wombs (*Deuteronomy 28:1,11:a).* We will carefully follow the terms of your covenant, so that we may prosper in everything we do (*Deuteronomy 29:9*). We are willing and obedient, so we will eat the fat from the land, hallelujah! (*Isaiah 1:19*). In Jesus' Name. Amen!

# PRIDE

*"Pride goeth before destruction, and an haughty spirit before a fall." Proverbs 16:18*

In 2 Chronicles 26:3-21, we saw that at 16 years old, Uzziah became King and reigned 52 years in Jerusalem.

Uzziah sought God and God made him prosper. He became strong in his heart and transgressed against God by entering the temple of the Lord to burn incense on the altar of incense. So Azariah the priest went in after him, and with him were eighty priests of the Lord, valiant men.

Back then, the priests who were consecrated to do so did the burn offering, so Azariah said, "It's not for you, Uzziah, to burn incense to the Lord, but for the priests, the sons of Aaron, who are consecrated to burn incense. Get out of the sanctuary, for you have trespassed; you shall have no honor from the Lord." Then Uzziah became furious (prideful), and he had a censer in his hand to burn incense. And while he was angry with the priests, leprosy broke out on his forehead, before the priests in the house of the Lord, beside the incense altar. And Azariah the chief priest and all the priests looked at him, and there, on his forehead, he was leprous; so they pushed him out of the place. Indeed he also hurried to get out, because the Lord had struck him. King Uzziah was a leper until the day of his death. He dwelt in an isolated house, because he was a leper; for he was cut off from the house of the Lord.

Pride is a result of the fall of man. Pride cost Adam and Eve their place in Paradise. Pride caused Lucifer to be cast out of heaven. Pride is a sin and we were born in sin so that is what entered in our hearts. Pride is when you are preoccupied with yourself. The only way to know if you are preoccupied with yourself is to always evaluate your motive. I am not ashamed to say I have challenges in this area from time to time, and God is working in and through me to rid me of this deadly sin. It is because of the grace of God that I am not consumed. We can become prideful in so many areas.

What are some of the reasons you become prideful? Admit that you have challenges with pride, submit them and yourself to God, and ask Him to help you to overcome in that area. He is faithful to do what you ask Him to do. I am learning that if God is not getting the glory, pride exists.

## *Prayer*
Lord, remind me that when pride comes, then comes disgrace. In Jesus' name. Amen!

# PRIDE
## LET'S TALK

*Thus says the Lord: "Let not the wise man glory in his wisdom, Let not the mighty man glory in his might, Nor let the rich man glory in his riches; But let him who glories glory in this, That he understands and knows Me, That I am the Lord, exercising lovingkindness, judgment, and righteousness in the earth. For in these I delight," says the Lord. Jeremiah 29:23-24*

How does one get rid of pride? I believe you get rid of pride by serious fasting and praying and employing the works of the Holy Spirit. We all know prideful people. I have been working with attorneys for over twenty-two plus years and let me tell you, I have worked with some proud attorneys and I have also worked with some humble attorneys. Pride shows up in our lives without us even realizing it. Pride is competitive by nature, meaning you'll stop at nothing to make sure you are always on the winning side because you don't want to look inferior. Being humble is a sure cure for pride.

**<u>TRANSPARENCY ALERT</u>**! Am I always humble? No, not all the time, but I know when I am prideful. The spirit in me convicts me. I submit to God and I repent. Pride creeps in every now and then. I just stopped for a minute and reflected on times I knew I was being prideful. I just need to master walking in the Spirit consistently and not fulfill the lust of the flesh. If you have mastered this, please share.

True humility is thanking God for our talents and gifts and giving Him credit for our accomplishments. Let us work on removing pride and replacing it with true humility, so help us Holy Ghost.

# PRAYER

Hallelujah. Hallelujah. Hallelujah! *Holiness, holiness....is what I long for Holiness is what I need Holiness, holiness Is what You want from me Take my life....and form it Take my mind...transform it Take my will...conform it To Yours, to Yours, Oh Lord

Lord Jesus, search me and reveal to me if I am (*2 Timothy 3:5*a) having a form of godliness but denying its power. Remind me daily, Holy Spirit that (*Romans 14:17*) the kingdom of God is not a matter of eating and drinking, but of righteousness, peace and joy in the Holy Spirit. (*I Corinthians 6:20*) For I am bought with a price; therefore I will continue to glorify God in my body, and in my spirit, which are God's. (*I*

*Corinthians 6:15*) I am reminded daily that my body is a member of Christ. (*I Peter 1:16*) For it is written: Be holy, because I am holy. (*Psalm 119:9*) How shall I cleanse my way? By taking heed thereto according to your word. Help me Holy Spirit to take heed to Your words so my ways and thoughts can be pure before Your eyes.

*Take My Life (Holiness) by Mercy Me (public domain)

## PROMISES-UNFULFILLED
## LET'S TALK

*"For all the promises of God in Him are Yes, and in Him Amen, to the glory of God through us."* II Corinthians 1:20

What is a promise? A promise is a declaration or assurance that one will do a particular thing.

**TRANSPARENCY ALERT**: God is constantly revealing the areas where growth is needed in my life. *"No discipline seems pleasant at the time, but painful. Later on, however, it produces a harvest of righteousness and peace for those who have been trained by it." Hebrews 12:11 NIV.*

How many promises have I broken? The one that I recently started working on is saying, "I'll call you later." Okay, what does *later* really mean? Does it mean later today, tomorrow or next month? I don't know. For me, when I say later, I mean that same day.

Have you ever made a promise to do something for someone with the right intentions, but was not able to follow through because something else came up or you forgot? **Pause for a minute and take a stroll down memory lane.** I have been there. I am learning not to be quick to say yes and that it is okay to say no, nicely.

That is the difference between us and God. God cannot go back on His word. There are over 8,600 promises in the bible for us from God. And guess what? His word will not return void. So on the basis of that truth and because we want to be people of integrity, here are some tips to help us keep our promises to others:

## _Tips_

1. Do not be too quick to make a promise or volunteer to do something.

   Learn to say no.

2. It's okay to say, I am not able to right now or I will get back in touch with you later.

3. You can also ask the question, how soon do you need an answer?

When we don't keep a promise to someone, it communicates to that person that we don't value him or her. Not good. When we break small promises, others learn that they cannot count on us. _"It is better **not** to make a vow than to make one and not fulfill it." (Ecclesiastes 5:5)._

# PUNCTUALITY

*"For Sarah conceived, and bare Abraham a son in his old age, at the set time of which God had spoken to him." Genesis 21:2*

There are so many reasons why we just cannot be punctual all the time. Let's look at some reasons: car accident, flat tire, woke up late, just don't care, sick child, wife and husband. The list goes on.

Can you think of a situation where you failed to be on time, but you should have been? What issue is in your life that would improve with increased punctuality? Do you use your schedule to glorify God and help others, or is it just a private matter where you are not concerned with time?

Think through the steps you need to take to put punctuality into action in a specific instance, such as, how can I make sure I keep my schedule focused on God's priorities and not just my own? How can I plan things out effectively, being prompt, yet not being bruised when they do not work out? What can I do to make sure I get to work on time?

## *Prayer*

Lord, help me to serve you by not being intentionally late. In Jesus' name. Amen!

# RACISM

*"For there is no respect of persons with God." Romans 2:11*

I grew up on the beautiful island of Jamaica and I never knew racism existed until I migrated to the United States. Even today, I still hear stories from others who are going through those experiences. To be racist is to not know who God is. Almost everyone knows of God, but does not truly know Him. Even though the world does not always treat humans as equals, as members of the body of Christ, all are equal spiritually in the eyes of Jesus.

If you are experiencing racism in the workplace or you are the one being racist, I encourage you to pray for yourself and that other racist person or persons from a true heart, and ask God to show

Himself strong on your behalf. Gather a few prayer warriors together and bombard heaven. Love has no color or race and God is love. He said in *Proverbs 21:1 "The king's heart is in the hand of the LORD, as the rivers of water: He turns it wherever He will."* So God will turn the heart of the racist. Keep praying and keep believing.

## *Prayer*

Lord, always remind me that there is neither Jew nor Greek, slave nor free, male nor female, for we are all one in Christ Jesus. In Jesus' name. Amen!

# REBELLION

*"For rebellion is as the sin of witchcraft, and stubbornness is as iniquity and idolatry. Because thou hast rejected the word of the Lord, he hath also rejected thee from being king." I Samuel 15:23*

In this story, King Saul allowed the people to intimidate him and in return he rebelled against the authority of God's command. The people also rebelled against the command of God when they intimidated Saul so that he would obey their will instead of God. In response to this rebellion, the scripture states that rebellion is as witchcraft.

Truth moment. (remember this is between you and God): Have you ever disobeyed God about one thing and you thought it was okay because you are pleasing Him in other ways? Do you consider yourself stubborn? We cannot look at these words the same again.

Stress and work environment can be major causes for rebellion and stubbornness.

What are some reasons you are stressed?

1. _____

2. _____

3. _____

4. _____

5. _____

Why do you feel you have to be stubborn?

1. _____

2. _____

3. _____

4. _____

5. _____

## *Prayer*

Lord, You said you have spread out Your hands all day long to a rebellious people, who walk in the way which is not good, following their own thoughts. Help me not to follow my own thoughts. In Jesus' name. Amen!

# RELATIONSHIP
## LET'S TALK

Right relationships between employers and employees are important because we spend so much time on the job. It is important for employers to respect their employees and just as important for employees to respect their employers.

Right relationship in the workplace causes an *increase in productivity*. When the relationship is right, it creates a pleasant atmosphere and increases the employees' motivation. Right relationship in the workplace causes *employees to show loyalty*. Creating a productive and pleasant work environment has a drastic effect on an employee's loyalty to the business/firm/organization.

Did you know that employees who respect their employer and employers who respect and value their employees cause employees to feel happy? And when they are happy, they tend to do more than is expected. I believe that is one of the key components to success for any business/ firm/ organization.

Wrong relationship in the workplace causes employees to **lose confidence in leadership**. When employees have lost confidence, they lose trust. Wrong relationship in the workplace causes employees to **lose motivation**. When employees are not motivated they do not perform to the best of their ability.

At that point when you have lost motivation and confidence in leadership, you pray the Holy Ghost brings back to remembrance the Word that says *"And whatever you do, do it heartily, as to the Lord and not to men, knowing that from the Lord you will receive the reward of the inheritance; for you serve the*

*Lord Christ.*" (Colossians 3:23-24). The Amplified Version read- "*Whatever you do [whatever your task may be], work from the soul [that is, put in your very best effort], as [something done] for the Lord and not for men, knowing [with all certainty] that it is from the Lord [not from men] that you will receive the inheritance which is your [greatest] reward. It is the Lord Christ whom you [actually] serve.*" The truth of the matter is, respect or no respect, we still have an obligation to God because He is who we must aim to please. We are working for God.

**SIDE NOTE**: You have to already know a verse of scripture in order for the Holy Ghost to bring it back to your memory.

# RESPECT

*"Honour all men. Love the brotherhood. Fear God. Honour the king." I Peter 2:17*

Sometimes it is not easy to respect others who we feel do not deserve to be respected. The good thing in that is, we are not going by what we feel. The truth is, sometimes, I don't feel saved, but I know I am. We are going by what the word of God says. I have learned that it does not matter how bad I think a person is.

There is always something I can find in that person to respect. This is just the awesomeness of Almighty God. He said in *I John 4:10 "This is love: not that we loved God, but that he loved us and sent his Son as an atoning sacrifice for our sins."* When we meditate on those words, we simply should not disrespect someone God loves. For God so loved the world; he loves everyone. We are commanded to respect others regardless of color, nationality, opinions or affiliations, etc.

## *Prayer*

Lord, help me to show respect from the least to the greatest by seeing everyone through Your eyes. In Jesus' name. Amen!

# SOWING AND REAPING

"*Be not deceived; God is not mocked: for whatsoever a man soweth, that shall he also reap.*" *Galatians 6:7*

Let's use a garden as an example. You can change almost anything, but you cannot change seedtime and harvest. If you don't plant, you cannot expect to reap. If you plant watermelon seed you will get watermelon. If you plan okra seed, you will reap okra (I love okra). Whatever seed you plant in the ground, you will reap the harvest for that seed.

In this instance, the garden is our heart. There are certain negative seeds we do not want in our garden, such as complaining, doubt, unbelief, defeat, hatred, bitterness, whining, argumentative and retaliation. Out of the abundance of our heart, our mouth will speak.

List some other negative seeds that you are thinking of right now.

1. _____

2. _____

3. _____

4. _____

5. _____

6. _____

7. _____

We will plant positive seeds of faith, hope, strength, health, forgiveness, humility and praise. We will fertilize them with joy, peace, love, encouragement and blessing, and you will reap a bountiful harvest. In whatever amount you sow, it will come back to you.

You are responsible for you. If you are sowing negative seeds on the job, ask God to help you to transform those negative seeds into positive seeds. Before you go to bed at night, reflect on your work day. I have been doing that quite a bit, Lord knows. Throughout the day, think about the seeds you have sown, whether in thoughts, words or deeds, and ask God to help you to not sow those same seeds going forward.

## *Prayer*

Lord, help me to not grow weary in doing good because I will reap if I faint not. In Jesus' name.

## AMEN!TEAMWORK

*"Two are better than one; because they have a good reward for their labour." Ecclesiastes 4:9*

If you have not seen the movie, Antz, I strongly recommend it. There is so much to learn from this movie. I watched it years ago when my daughter was 2 or 3 years old, and that movie came back to me as I thought about what to write for this topic. The Ants live and work together in highly organized societies called colonies. Each individual ant has a tiny brain, but all the ants of a colony combined are pretty smart. Ant super-organisms can solve difficult problems by processing information as a group, not individually but collectively.

When we work together for the betterment of the firm/company/organization, etc., and not fight each other, we can be very successful. Not everyone works well in a group; some work best alone. I think about all the researchers who are trying to find a cure for cancer. Can you imagine if they ALL would get together and just share their information? I think the cure is already out there, but they need a little bit from each other's research to complete the puzzle. We are living in a power-driven society, where I need to be the one to come out on top. I need to be the one to get ALL the credit.

## *The Wonder Pets- I love their song. This is the chorus:*

"Wonder Pets! Wonder Pets! We're on our wayTo help a baby [animal] and save the day!" Ming-Ming: "We're not too big," Tuck: "And we're not too tough," All: "But when we work together we've got the right stuff! Go, Wonder Pets! Yay"

That is my song. When someone is super busy and you are not, ask if you can assist. Can you remember a time someone helped you out in a big way or you helped someone out in a big way with a project?

## _Prayer_

Lord, bless the work of my hands and cause me to always be willing to lend a helping hand when needed. In Jesus' name. Amen!

*Wonder Pets by _Josh Selig_ (public domain)

# TEMPTATION

*"There hath no temptation taken you but such as is common to man: but God is faithful, who will not suffer you to be tempted above that ye are able; but will with the temptation also make a way to escape, that ye may be able to bear it." 1 Corinthians 10:13*

We are tempted daily and we will be tempted until we die. We are tempted to curse someone out on the job.... let's be honest now. We are tempted to cut corners. What are some of the ways you are tempted? Think about it.

David was tempted and yielded (in 2 Samuel 11:4) and Joseph was tempted and fled for his life (in Genesis 39:13-18). The grace of God enabled Joseph to overcome the temptation by avoiding the tempter. He did not stay to play around with the temptation, but fled from it, as escaping for his life. If we mean not to do iniquity, let us flee as a deer from the hunter.

Temptation does not necessarily mean cheating. Temptation comes in many forms in the workplace. You know when you are tempted to do something you shouldn't. That feeling in your heart that is saying don't do it----that is God convicting you before you yield. Sometimes we completely ignore that still small voice. Sometimes our hearts become hardened and our conscience so smeared that we don't even hear or feel that a thing is wrong. But thanks be to God who causes us to triumph.

## *Prayer*

Lord, remind me that when I am tempted, I am drawn away by my own desires and enticed, because when desire has conceived, it gives birth to sin; and sin, when it is full-grown, brings forth death. In Jesus' name. Amen!

# THANKSGIVING

*"Enter into his gates with thanksgiving, and into his courts with praise: be thankful unto him, and bless his name." Psalm 100:4*

Thanksgiving is a holiday that we look forward to. It is a day out of the year that we come together to eat, whether it is with family or friends. The truth of the matter is, every day is a day of thanksgiving. The fact that we woke up in our right minds is something to be thankful for. We take a lot for granted because just about everything is at our finger tips.

A couple of years ago, our HVAC went out during the summer and we had to sleep with the windows open. This was our first time without AC. We usually ran our AC all day, every day during the summer months. During that season, I experienced something I had never experienced since we relocated to NC. I felt God's sweet breeze coming through the windows. It felt so good. I kept saying "wow, this is nice". I could not remember the last time I was so thankful for a cool breeze.

We are reminded to give thanks in everything because it is the will of God for us in Christ. Sometimes we allow the cares of the world to blind us. I know if you really think about it, no matter what is going on in the world or with us, personally, we can find something to give God thanks for. We really can. So, I am challenging you to find something to be thankful for in the midst of the challenges you are now facing.

## *Prayer*

Lord, help me to see you in everything and give you thanks all the time. In Jesus' name. Amen!

# THANKSGIVING-CHALLENGE

*"In everything give thanks: for this is the will of God in Christ Jesus concerning you." I Thessalonians 5:18*

It is so easy for us to say thank you when someone gives us a gift or does something wonderful for us. I challenge you to find seven (7) things every day, regarding your job, that you are thankful for. Every day is really a day of thanksgiving even if you are thankful for the same seven (7) things.

1. _____

2. _____

3. _____

4. _____

5. _____

6. _____

7. _____

## *Prayer*

Help me to always give thanks to the LORD, for He is good; His love endures forever. In Jesus' name. Amen!

# TRUST

*"It is better to trust in the Lord than to put confidence in man." Psalm 118:8*

There are so many things we are trusting God for these days. If you start a list, I bet it would be very long. Some of the things we are trusting God for are good health, financial security, daily provision, a house, car, dream vacation, protection, a baby, spouse or even a great-paying job. Have you ever said to Him, Lord, I am trusting you to help me to be the best employee ever? It sounds corny, doesn't it? But in fact, it is not.

There are days I feel like I did my best, but then felt like my best was just not good enough. There is absolutely nothing wrong with trusting God for your dream vacation to Hawaii. I have been trusting him for that for over 14 years, and I still believe it will happen in the fullness of time. When I told Him I was trusting Him to help me to be the best employee ever, I know He smiled at me.

I acknowledge that this is not something I can do in my own strength. It is really going to require divine intervention on my behalf. God asked us to "trust in Him with ALL our hearts and to not lean on our own understanding, but to acknowledge Him in all our ways, so He can direct our path." He is not a man, that He should lie. Whatever He says, He will do. I know He will show Himself strong on my behalf.

What are some things you are trusting God for in the workplace? Clearly, you already have an idea of all I am trusting God for, by way of the various topics mentioned.

## *Prayer*

Lord, help me to trust in You at all times, to pour out my heart to You, for You are my refuge. In Jesus' name. Amen!

# UNFORGIVENESS
## LET'S TALK

*"And be ye kind one to another, tenderhearted, forgiving one another, even as God for Christ's sake hath forgiven you." Ephesians 4:32*

We have all been hurt/disappointed at some point or another in our lives. Truth be told, you also have done some hurting and disappointing over the years as well. This subject of unforgiveness is dear to my heart, because I know certain situations can leave deep wounds in our spirits. But thank God for the blood of Jesus Christ, and knowing that forgiveness is not for the person who might have hurt us, but for us. Hallelujah!

Forgiveness doesn't mean forgetting the offense. Pretending the wrong never happened prevents healing. We must learn to say "I forgive you." "Please forgive me." As you pray these different prayers, please personalize and pray them for yourself as well.

**TRANSPARENCY ALERT**! In 2015, I had a few face-to-face encounters, sent emails and sent text messages (15 people total) asking for forgiveness. I had to humble myself, ask the Holy Spirit to help me and ask these individuals for forgiveness. I go to God all the time throughout the day, asking for forgiveness when I get a wrong thought or say something that was not pleasing to His ears. I am reminded of *Psalm 139 1-4 "O Lord, You have searched me and known me. You know my sitting down and my rising up; You understand my thought afar off. You comprehend my path and my lying down, And are acquainted with all my ways. For there is not a word on my tongue, But behold, O Lord, You know it altogether."*

This is why I have to ask Him to forgive me. So if you are reading this and I have offended you, please forgive me. Do you know you can offend others without knowing? You sure can.

## *Prayer*

Lord, I know unforgiveness is as the sin of witchcraft. Help me to not harbor unforgiveness so my blessings can flow easily. In Jesus' name. Amen!

# PRAYER

Hallelujah. Hallelujah. Hallelujah. Glory. Thank You Jesus. We bless, honor and magnify Your Holy Name on this new day that will soon pass. Hallelujah is the highest praise. Hallelujah. Hallelujah. Hallelujah.

(*Romans 8:18*) ...consider that the sufferings of this present time are not worthy to be compared with the glory which shall be revealed in us. (*Rom 8:37*) Yet in all these things, we are more than conquerors through Him who loved us. (*Romans 8:39*) We know that nothing can separate us from the love of God which is in Christ Jesus our Lord. (*Romans 8:28*) We know that all things work together for good to those who love God, to those who are the called according to His purpose. (*2 Timothy 4:5*) We are watchful in all things, endure afflictions, do the work of an evangelist, fulfill our ministry. (*2 Timothy 4:7*) We will pray for each other daily and continue to fight the good fight, finish the race, keep the faith. (*Micah 7:8*) Do not rejoice over me, my enemy; when I fall, I will arise; when I sit in darkness, the Lord will be a light to me, in your face Satan. (*Philippians 4:13*) We can do all things through Christ who strengthens us. Lord, thank you for reminding us of your word continually that says (*1 John 4:4*) We have overcome them, because He who is in us is greater than he that is in the world. (*Philippians 1:6*) We are confident of this very thing, that He who has begun a good work in us will complete it until the day of Jesus Christ. (*Philippians 4:4*) We will rejoice in the Lord always.

Again I say, rejoice! Hallelujah. Hallelujah. Hallelujah. Glory! Thank You Jesus. We are standing firm on Your promises.

Glory. Hallelujah. Hallelujah!

# WORRY

*"Cast thy burden upon the Lord, and he shall sustain thee: he shall never suffer the righteous to be moved."*
*Psalm 55:22*

Luke 10:38-42: Now it happened as they went that He entered a certain village; and a certain woman named Martha welcomed Him into her house. And she had a sister called Mary, who also sat at Jesus' feet and heard His word. But Martha was distracted with much serving, and she approached Him and said, "Lord, do You not care that my sister has left me to serve alone? Therefore tell her to help me." And Jesus answered and said to her, "Martha, Martha, you are worried and troubled about many things. But one thing is needed, and

Mary has chosen that good part, which will not be taken away from her."

On the job, we worry about deadlines, not billing enough time, downsizing, layoffs, how to please our bosses. Worry breeds stress. When some people are stressed out they eat, which leads to weight gain, while others lose their appetite and loses weight. Worry can cause you to be physically sick, and sickness breathes hospital and doctor bills. Who wants those? Yours truly was a worry hog. I am learning daily to cast all my cares upon the Lord. Worry does not change any situation, but prayer does. There are times I find myself worrying about the future, just not knowing what is ahead. We all have been in a situation that caused us to worry at some point in our lives. Worrying is not the life our Father wants for us. I dare you to not worry about the next situation that will come up. Another thing to remember is that worry wipes out faith because we ought to walk by faith and not by sight.

## *Prayer*

Lord, help me to cast all my cares upon You; for You care for me. In Jesus' name. Amen!

# ZEAL

*"Who gave himself for us, that he might redeem us from all iniquity, and purify unto himself a peculiar people, zealous of good works." Titus 2:14*

Zacchaeus was a wealthy and determined Tax Collector who was zealous for the things of God. (Luke 19:1-10). It was so intense that when heard that Jesus was coming through his neighborhood, he climbed a sycamore-fig tree. His determination caused Jesus to say, okay, come down, I must stay at your house today. Can you imagine the feeling that came over Zaccheaus after Jesus said those words? After his encounter with Jesus, he boiled over with zeal. What did Zaccheaus tell Jesus he would do? How did Jesus respond?

Let us go down memory lane. Do you remember your first paying job? You had that zeal to get up every day, show up on time, get your work done, get your pay at the end of the week, and you were excited to go back to work the following week. You were especially looking forward to that paycheck, so that was your motivation to be zealous about work.

Over time, something happened along the way. You became discouraged. It is easy to lose your zeal based on circumstance surrounding your job to the point where getting a paycheck does not motivate you anymore. You dread going into work and you feel like what is the point. Same old same old. Have you ever had those feelings? Been there.

Well, guess what? There is a cure for that. Think back to when you lost your zeal and determine what was taking place at the time you felt your zeal decreasing. I do believe that zeal can be rekindled, but it is up to you. No one can rekindle it for you.

You have to be transformed by the renewing of your mind. To regain that zeal, you first must have a burning desire to please God on the job. That is the start. We have to be wholehearted in serving God in the workplace. Put aside everything negative that comes to your mind to make you feel like you do not want to perform your best. Talk to God about your situation and trust Him to help you to deal with it and get your zeal back. I dare you to trust Him today.

## *Prayer*

Lord, I thank you for giving me the fervor that I once experienced. In Jesus' name. Amen!

# END PRAYER

Hallelujah. Hallelujah. Hallelujah. Wonderful Jesus, Prince of Peace, Lilly of the Valley, Bright and Morning Star, Alpha and Omega, the Beginning and the End, the First and the Last, my Bridge over troubled waters, I lift You up. Hallelujah! Hallelujah!

Thank You for inspiring my heart, mind and spirit so I could complete this workplace devotion. To You alone be the glory, praise and honor. Thank You for helping my readers and I to see the workplace as You see it. Remind us daily who we are working for. Help us to face each day with a new attitude and plenty of gratitude and to see each other through Your eyes.

Lord, we acknowledge that we cannot do this without You. Continue to be our guide on this journey so we can hear, well done, though good and faithful servant. These mercies I ask, in no other name, but Jesus' name. Amen!

# QUESTIONS

What are some challenges you encounter in the workplace?

How are you dealing with those areas?

Is God a part of your solution to the different challenges?

Do you think you are where you are for the rest of your life?

Are you happy on your job?

If you are not, why are you still there?

Are you working as unto the Lord?

What has God called you to do?

Are you seeking God's direction for your future?

Do you have a vision for yourself regarding where you would like to work and what you would like to be doing?

Now that you know that God is your Boss, how are you going to change your attitude toward the workplace going forward?

What steps are you going to take?

# QUOTES
## BY CHARLEEN L. GOOMBS

My Christian life does not mean I am happy all the time. I have moments of discouragement. Those moments keep me humble before my all-knowing God. It is then I pray, Lord, have mercy on me.

Brokenness and humility cause me to hear from God more clearly. When I am filled with pride and haughtiness, I cannot hear a thing.

If we listen to someone intently, we can hear what is not being said.

Do not be deceived, thinking all the work we do in our ministry and all the financial contributions we give will get us into heaven. Good works cannot buy our way into heaven; being a doer of the Word and not only a hearer, will.

We cannot fathom the depth of God if we don't meditate on His Word day and night, and allow Him to reveal Himself to us by His Spirit.

A grateful heart pushes out the spirit of murmuring and complaining.

God does not see us as others see us and as we see ourselves. When He looks at us, He smiles because we are His workmanship.

There is a problem when we put someone on a pedestal instead of God. If that someone falls off the pedestal, we will likely be disappointed and then start judging. God never falls off His pedestal, so there is no room for disappointment in Him.

Do not beat others over the head for not thinking the way you think, loving the way you love, and acting the way you act, because at the end of the day, in God's eyes you are both the same. Whose eyes are you seeing others through?

It does not matter how unkind and selfish you think a person is. If you have several conversations with that person long enough, you will find some good.

When we feel lost, we can always find our way because God is the way, the truth, and the life.

You cannot warfare successfully if your hobby is watching T.V. Remember, deep calleth unto deep.

Sometimes you have to separate yourself from the ones you love for a season so God can reveal things to you by His spirit.

Other people's opinion of me is not God's truth.

Unemployment is not the end of your life. It is the beginning of a bright future. *"For I know the thoughts that I think toward you, saith the Lord, thoughts of peace, and not of evil, to give you an expected end." Jeremiah 29:11.*

Christians love to ask others if they are believers. Are you a believer? If the answer is yes, then your next question should be, a believer of what or who? Everyone is a believer of something or someone.

## ABOUT CHARLEEN

Proud wife, mother and devoted servant of God, whose desire is to follow as God leads, humble herself under His mighty hand, and allow Him to use her for His glory by being a positive example of His Word and His Love to **_all_** who come across her path.

Charleen blesses God by giving Him all the praise, glory and honor for what He has done and will continue to do in her life, by showing Himself strong on her behalf as she continues to acknowledge Him in all of her ways so He can direct her path. She never wants to forget where she is coming from, because in remembering, she will always give God the glory. She continues to fight the good fight of faith daily with a desire to "lean not on her own understanding."

# CONTACT INFORMATION

To contact Charleen L. Goombs, e-mail her at

charleengoombs@gmail.com

www.ingramcontent.com/pod-product-compliance
Lightning Source LLC
LaVergne TN
LVHW041214080426
835508LV00011B/951